CIPS STUDY MATTERS

ADVANCED CERTIFICATE
IN PROCUREMENT AND SUPPLY OPERATIONS

COURSE BOOK

Procurement and Supply Operations

© Profex Publishing Limited, 2016

Printed and distributed by:

The Chartered Institute of Procurement & Supply,
Easton House, Easton on the Hill, Stamford, Lincolnshire PE9 3NZ
Tel: +44 (0) 1780 756 777
Fax: +44 (0) 1780 751 610
Email: info@cips.org
Website: www.cips.org

First edition September 2012
Reprinted with minor amendments June 2016

All rights reserved. No part of this publication may be reproduced, stored in a retrieval system or transmitted, in any form or by any means, electronic, mechanical, photocopying, recording or otherwise, without the written permission of Profex Publishing Limited.

While every effort has been made to ensure that references to websites are correct at time of going to press, the world wide web is a constantly changing environment and neither CIPS nor Profex Publishing Limited can accept responsibility for any changes to addresses.

We acknowledge product, service and company names referred to in this publication, many of which are trade names, service marks, trademarks or registered trademarks.

CIPS, The Chartered Institute of Procurement & Supply, and its logo, are all trademarks of The Chartered Institute of Procurement & Supply.

Contents

		Page
	Preface	v
	The Unit Content	vii
	How to Use Your Course Book	ix
1	**Obtaining Supplies**	1

The five rights of procurement; sources of added value; value for money; products and services

2	**The Right Price**	15

What is the right price?; suppliers' approaches to pricing; the link between costs and prices; using competition to obtain quotations; measuring achieved savings

3	**Achieving Quality Supplies**	35

The right quality; costs of quality; managing supplier quality; quality control; quality assurance; total quality management

4	**The Right Quantity at the Right Time**	53

Inventories and their costs; forecasting demand; scheduling; lead times; managing supplier delivery performance

5	**Identifying Procurement Needs**	71

Liaison with users and customers; buyer and supplier contributions; information requirements for specification development; influences on specification development; the make/do or buy decision

6	**Creating Specifications**	85

Specifications and tolerances; the importance of specifications; types of specification; specifying services; the role of KPIs

7	**Sourcing and Selecting Suppliers**	99

Surveying the market; criteria for supplier appraisal; information for supplier appraisal; measuring supplier performance

Page

8 Formation of Agreements — 113

Formation of contracts; the contracting process; transparency and fairness

9 Electronic P2P Systems — 125

The procurement cycle; identify and define requirements; identify and select potential suppliers; monitor, review and maintain performance; procure-to-pay systems (P2P); integration of systems between organisations

10 Internet Technologies in Procurement — 141

IT and procurement; communicating via the internet; web-based solutions; data to smooth demand and supply

Subject Index — 149

Preface

Welcome to your new Course Book.

Your Course Book provides detailed coverage of all topics specified in the unit content.

For a full explanation of how to use your new Course Book, turn now to page ix. And good luck in your studies!

A note on style

Throughout your Course Books you will find that we use the masculine form of personal pronouns. This convention is adopted purely for the sake of stylistic convenience – we just don't like saying 'he/she' all the time. Please don't think this reflects any kind of bias or prejudice.

June 2016

The Unit Content

The unit content is reproduced below, together with reference to the chapter in this Course Book where each topic is covered.

Unit purpose and aim(s)

On completion of this unit, candidates will be able to identify a range of considerations in formulating agreements with external organisations.

This unit assesses procurement and supply operations and is structured around the achievement of the five rights namely price, quality, time, quantity and place.

Learning outcomes, assessment criteria and indicative content

Chapter

1.0 Understand the main techniques that can achieve added value through procurement operations

1.1 Explain techniques to obtain supplies to the purchaser's requirements

- The five rights of procurement — 1
- Defining sources of added value — 1
- Defining value for money — 1
- Applying the five rights to procurements of both products and services — 1

1.2 Analyse techniques to secure competitive pricing

- Using competition to obtain quotations on prices — 2
- Comparing prices quoted to historical data — 2
- Suppliers' approaches to pricing — 2
- The link between costs and prices — 2
- Negotiating improved prices — 2
- Securing competitive pricing through competition or collaboration with suppliers — 2
- Measuring achieved savings — 2

1.3 Explain techniques to achieve quality supplies

- Defining quality — 3
- Quality standards, processes and procedures — 3
- The use of quality assurance — 3
- The concept of zero defects — 3
- Assessing quality of supplies of products and services — 3

1.4 Assess techniques to secure required quantities at required timescales

- Internal, external and total lead time — 4
- Expediting and measuring delivery performance — 4
- Planning milestones and activities — 4
- The use of scheduling — 4
- Inventories and their costs — 4

Chapter

2.0 Understand the main tasks associated with each stage of the sourcing process

2.1 Explain how procurement needs are identified

- Liaison with users and customers and understanding their commercial needs — 5
- Reviewing needs from customers — 5
- The make or buy decision — 5
- Definitions of specifications — 5

2.2 Explain criteria that should be applied in creating specifications

- The importance of specifications in contracts with external customers and suppliers — 6
- Creating specifications for products and services — 6
- Conformance and output or outcome based approaches to developing specifications — 6
- The role of key performance indicators (KPIs) — 6

2.3 Assess approaches to the sourcing of supplies

- Surveying the market — 7
- Supplier appraisal — 7
- Inviting quotations and tenders — 2
- Assessing quotations and tenders — 2
- The use of e-sourcing technologies — 10
- Measuring supplier performance — 7

2.4 Explain approaches to the formation of agreements with external organisations

- Dealing with queries and clarifications — 8
- Ensuring transparency and fairness with suppliers — 8
- Mistakes and second bids in tenders — 8
- The use of reverse auctions/e-auctions — 8
- Forming agreements with customers and suppliers — 8
- Transition and mobilisation arrangements — 8

3.0 Understand the impact of technology on procurement operations

3.1 Explain the impact of electronic procure to pay (P2P) systems on procurement operations

- The stages of the sourcing process from identification of needs to the award of agreements — 9
- Creating approvals and their timescales — 9
- Defining procure to pay (P2P) systems — 9
- Automating requisitions, purchase orders and invoices — 9
- Integration of systems between organisations — 9

3.2 Explain how the use of internet technologies can support procurement operations

- Providing data to smooth demand and supply — 10
- Communicating via the internet — 10
- Web-based solutions such as e-requisitioning, e-sourcing, e-ordering, e-invoicing — 10

How to Use Your Course Book

Organising your study

'Organising' is the key word: unless you are a very exceptional student, you will find a haphazard approach is insufficient, particularly if you are having to combine study with the demands of a full-time job.

A good starting point is to timetable your studies, in broad terms, between now and the date of your assessment. How many subjects are you attempting? How many chapters are there in the Course Book for each subject? Now do the sums: how many days/weeks do you have for each chapter to be studied?

Remember:

- Not every week can be regarded as a study week – you may be going on holiday, for example, or there may be weeks when the demands of your job are particularly heavy. If these can be foreseen, you should allow for them in your timetabling.
- You also need a period leading up to the assessment in which you will revise and practise what you have learned.

Once you have done the calculations, make a week-by-week timetable for yourself for each paper, allowing for study and revision of the entire unit content between now and the date of your assessment.

Getting started

Aim to find a quiet and undisturbed location for your study, and plan as far as possible to use the same period each day. Getting into a routine helps avoid wasting time. Make sure you have all the materials you need before you begin – keep interruptions to a minimum.

Using the Course Book

You should refer to the Course Book to the extent that you need it.

- If you are a newcomer to the subject, you will probably need to read through the Course Book quite thoroughly. This will be the case for most students.
- If some areas are already familiar to you – either through earlier studies or through your practical work experience – you may choose to skip sections of the Course Book.

The content of the Course Book

This Course Book has been designed to give detailed coverage of every topic in the unit content. As you will see from pages vii–viii, each topic mentioned in the unit content is dealt with in a chapter of the Course Book. For the most part the order of the Course Book follows the order of the unit content closely, though departures from this principle have occasionally been made in the interest of a logical learning order.

Each chapter begins with a reference to the assessment criteria and indicative content to be covered in the chapter. Each chapter is divided into sections, listed in the introduction to the chapter, and for the most part being actual captions from the unit content.

All of this enables you to monitor your progress through the unit content very easily and provides reassurance that you are tackling every subject that is assessable.

Each chapter contains the following features.

- An introduction
- Clear coverage of each topic in a concise and approachable format
- A chapter summary
- Self-test questions

The study phase

For each chapter you should begin by glancing at the main headings (listed at the start of the chapter). Then read fairly rapidly through the body of the text to absorb the main points. If it's there in the text, you can be sure it's there for a reason, so try not to skip unless the topic is one you are familiar with already.

Then return to the beginning of the chapter to start a more careful reading. You may want to take brief notes as you go along.

Test your recall and understanding of the material by attempting the self-test questions. These are accompanied by cross-references to paragraphs where you can check your answers and refresh your memory.

The revision phase

Your approach to revision should be methodical and you should aim to tackle each main area of the unit content in turn. Re-read your notes. Then do some question practice. The CIPS website contains many past exam questions and you should aim to identify those that are suitable for the unit you are studying.

Additional reading

Your Course Book provides you with the key information needed for each module but CIPS strongly advocates reading as widely as possible to augment and reinforce your understanding. CIPS produces an official reading list of books, which can be downloaded from the bookshop area of the CIPS website.

To help you, we have identified one essential textbook for each subject. We recommend that you read this for additional information.

The essential textbook for this unit is *Purchasing and Supply Chain Management* by Kenneth Lysons and Brian Farrington.

Examination

This unit is assessed by means of 60 multiple choice questions (MCQs) in a two-hour exam. For each question you must select one correct answer from four options. There will be 20 MCQs testing each of the three learning outcomes. The pass mark is 75%, so you must get at least 45 questions right.

CHAPTER 1
Obtaining Supplies

Assessment criteria and indicative content

1.1 Explain techniques to obtain supplies to the purchaser's requirements
- The five rights of procurement
- Defining sources of added value
- Defining value for money
- Applying the five rights to procurements of both products and services

Section headings

1. The five rights of procurement
2. Sources of added value
3. Value for money
4. Products and services

Introduction

The 'five rights of procurement' is a phrase used to convey the key objectives pursued by buyers. We begin this chapter by outlining the five rights.

We then go on to examine how buyers can add value and achieve value for money.

Finally, we explain how the five rights apply in the purchase of both tangible products and intangible services.

1 The five rights of procurement

Introduction to the five rights

1.1 The five rights are a traditional formula expressing the basic objectives of procurement, and the general criteria by which procurement performance is measured. Even if they are not called 'five rights', they are often covered in procurement literature as 'key procurement variables' (as in Baily et al) or 'procurement factors' (as in Lysons & Farrington). Essentially, we are all talking about the same thing – and the syllabus uses the five rights 'captions' in its assessment criteria. We will therefore give a brief overview of their nature and importance here.

1.2 The five rights (or five Rs) of procurement, and the importance of achieving them, are summarised in Table 1.1. Don't worry if you don't understand all the points or terminology yet: we will be discussing these matters in much more detail in subsequent chapters of this Course Book. But it may help to have a general idea, at this stage, or to come back to for integrative learning and revision.

Table 1.1 *The five rights of procurement*

RIGHT	DESCRIPTION	IMPORTANCE
Quality	Obtaining goods which are of satisfactory quality and fit for their purpose (suited to internal and external customer's needs), by: • Accurate specification of requirement and quality standards • Supplier- and buyer-side quality management	If not achieved: • Stock may have to be rejected or scrapped • Production machinery may be damaged • Finished products may be defective and have to be scrapped or re-worked • Defective products may reach customers, resulting in recalls, returns, compensation claims, lost goodwill, damaged reputation • The firm will incur high costs
Quantity	Obtaining goods in sufficient quantity to meet demand and maintain service levels while minimising excess stock holding (which incurs costs and risks), by: • Demand forecasting • Inventory management • Stock replenishment systems	If not achieved: • Insufficient stock may be held to meet demand. Stockouts may cause bottlenecks or shutdowns in production; costs of idle time; late delivery to customers; lost credibility, goodwill and sales • Excess stock may be ordered and/or held: tying up capital in 'idle' stock; wasting storage space; risking deterioration, theft or damage; risking obsolescence or disuse; incurring 'holding costs'
Place	Having goods delivered to the appropriate delivery point, packaged and transported in such a way as to secure their safe arrival in good condition, by: • Distribution planning • Transport planning • Packaging	If not achieved: • Goods may be delivered to the wrong place, creating delay and correction costs • Goods may be subject to unnecessary transport and handling (and related costs) • Goods may be damaged, contaminated or stolen in transit • Transport may cause unnecessary environmental damage
Time	Securing delivery of goods at the right time to meet demand, but not so early as to incur unnecessary inventory costs, by: • Demand management • Supplier management	If not achieved: • Goods may be too late, causing production bottlenecks (and associated costs) and/or delays in delivery to customers (with costs of damages, lost business) • Goods may be too early, causing undue risks and costs of holding inventory
Price	Securing all of the above at a price which is reasonable, fair, competitive and affordable. Ideally, minimising procurement costs in order to maximise profit, by: • Price analysis • Supplier cost analysis • Competitive pricing and negotiation	If not achieved: • Suppliers will be free to charge what they like, without check • Supplier profit margins will be 'squeezed' unfairly, leading to insecurity of supply • Materials and supply costs will rise • Profits will fall – or prices charged to customers will have to rise (losing sales) • There will be less profit to motivate shareholders and reinvest in the business

1.3 While achieving the five rights may be *essential* for effective procurement, it may not be *sufficient* for the organisation's objectives and aspirations. There may be additional objectives to consider.

- **Relationship development**: developing collaborative long-term relationships with suppliers, not just for the immediate supply contract, but for ongoing partnership and mutual advantage

- **Innovation and development**: not just 'right quality' now, but potential to come up with innovative products and processes, and make collaborative quality improvements over time
- **Ethics and corporate social responsibility**: ethical trading, social sustainability (eg using small local suppliers) and environmental protection (eg procurement of environmentally friendly supplies) – which may not always be compatible with 'right price', for example.
- **Total costs of ownership** of purchased items (especially large capital items such as machinery and equipment): not just 'right price' (purchase price), but the best total value package, including costs of installation, training, maintenance and repair, upgrading, insurance and so on.

1.4 It is especially worth noting that the five rights formula doesn't include 'the right supplier' – although selection of the right supplier will be crucial in achieving the other procurement objectives. Arguably, the 'right supplier' is one who can deliver the right quantity and quality to the right place at the right time at the right price. However, there may be other considerations in the choice of supplier, such as the supplier's compatibility with the buying organisation; its credibility and reliability; its potential for innovation and development; its willingness to commit to continuous improvement and relationship development; its ethical and environmental performance; and so on.

Interrelationships and trade-offs between the five rights

1.5 It is also important to realise that the five rights are interdependent and interlinked, in all sorts of ways. Sometimes you can't get one without the other, and sometimes you can't get both at the same time! Here are some examples.

- If you don't get the right quality, you aren't getting the right quantity (because some items will be rejected or scrapped), at the right time (because delays will be caused by inspections and re-works), or the right price (because poor quality does not represent value for money, and incurs costs).
- On the other hand, high quality goods take a longer time to specify, produce and inspect (to manage the quality) – and if you don't get goods at the 'right time', high quality may be irrelevant: you may already have disrupted production and disappointed customers. Some corners may need to be cut on quality for 'urgent' requirements.
- The concepts of right quantity and right time are highly interdependent. You can have large quantities delivered early, in order to be sure to have sufficient items in stock – or you can have small 'top up' quantities delivered at the last minute, when you have a more accurate idea of demand (or even in response to demand, in a just in time system).
- There is often a trade-off between the right price and the other rights. Higher quality specifications cost more, as do short lead times (or 'urgent' orders) and complex delivery requirements (eg multiple deliveries). Quantity is a more complex trade-off. In terms of acquisition costs, frequent small orders may actually cost more (because of the extra transaction and transport costs) than fewer, large orders (subject to bulk discounts). However, fewer, larger orders will incur higher stock holding costs (such as storage and insurance). So the quantity/time factor will also have to juggle price considerations.
- Failure in any one aspect will impact on the others – and on Procurement's overall performance.

Good practice

1.6 'Good practice' is simply:

- A technique, method, process or procedure that is believed to be effective and efficient at delivering desired outcomes.
- An effective and efficient way of achieving a task, based on learnable and repeatable procedures that have proven themselves in practice, over time and in a range of contexts.

1.7 By using 'the right methods' (which you might add to your list of procurement Rs), you are likely to achieve objectives with fewer problems, unforeseen complications, risks and wastes. You don't have to 're-invent the wheel' or solve common problems afresh each time. You can be confident you are doing 'the right things' in 'the right ways'.

1.8 Good practice in procurement therefore includes a range of activities, decision rules, processes and procedures that are designed to help purchasers to achieve the optimum mix of the five rights, and other procurement objectives. We will look at a range of these policies, procedures and practices as we proceed to look at the five rights – and the procurement cycle – throughout this Course Book.

2 Sources of added value

Competitive advantage

2.1 Professor Michael Porter argued that competitive advantage comes from the value a company creates for its customers. Value is the 'worth' of the product or service: what it costs the organisation to produce and what the customer is willing to pay for it. In other words:

- A firm creates value – by performing its activities better, differently or more efficiently than its competitors.
- Customers purchase value – measured by comparing a firm's products and services with those of its competitors.

2.2 The term 'added value' refers to a product acquiring greater value or worth as a result of all the processes that support it. Customer service is an obvious example, but it is possible to see the concept of adding value from a number of different perspectives.

Perspectives on added value

2.3 According to Porter, the ultimate value a firm creates is measured by the amount customers are willing to pay for its products or services above the cost to the firm of carrying out all its value-creating activities (production, service, logistics, marketing and so on). A firm is profitable if the realised value to customers (what they are prepared to pay) exceeds the collective cost of the firm's value-creating activities.

2.4 From an accounting perspective, therefore, added value is total revenue minus total costs of all activities undertaken to develop and market a product or service. This expresses the amount of economic value that has been added to the organisation's resources: how efficiently they are being used and how effectively they are being leveraged. From this perspective, you can add value either by inducing customers to pay more or by reducing costs. Seen from the customer's perspective, it means selling an equivalent product at lower prices (while maintaining viable profit margins), or providing additional product features or services to attract a premium price.

2.5 Value addition can be achieved through cost reduction or process efficiency. One of the most effective ways is to reduce the order cycle time by getting the goods to the market faster: this could be achieved by developing a well-managed and controlled supply chain that minimises waste and costs.

Porter's value chain model

2.6 The value chain is the sequence of business activities by which value is added to the products or services produced by an organisation or supply chain. It embraces the entire process from raw materials to finished delivered product and continuing after-sales service.

2.7 The value chain concept may be used to identify and understand specific potential sources of a firm's (or supply chain's) competitive advantage. The value chain separates out the strategically important activities of the business, in order to gain fuller understanding of the value of each.

2.8 Porter's value chain model shows total value as a combination of the value added by the activities of a business unit: Figure 1.1. (Note that these value adding activities are not the same as business functions: they may be carried out across departments.)

Figure 1.1 *Porter's value chain*

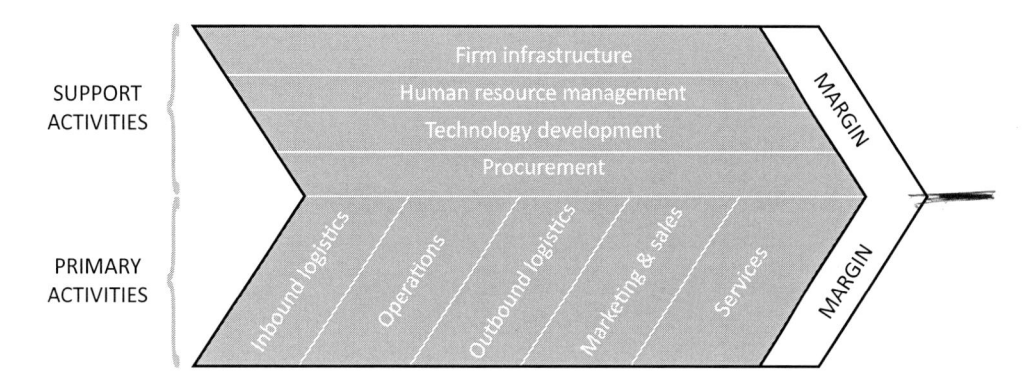

2.9 Primary value activities are grouped into five areas.
- Inbound logistics are the activities concerned with receiving, storing and disseminating inputs: materials handling, warehousing, inventory control etc.
- Operations are concerned with the transformation of inputs into finished goods or services. In manufacturing, these activities include assembly, testing, packing and equipment maintenance; in service industries, basic service provision.
- Outbound logistics are concerned with storing, distributing and delivering the finished goods to customers: warehousing, materials handling, transport planning, order processing and so on.
- Marketing and sales are responsible for communication with the customers to provide a means by which they can purchase the product (as well as an inducement to do so): market research, new product development, advertising and promotion, sales force management, channel management, pricing and so on.
- Service covers all of the activities which occur after the point of sale to enhance or maintain the value of the product for the customer: installation, repair, training, parts supply and maintenance.

2.10 The secondary, or support, activities operate across the primary activities, as in the case of procurement where at each stage items are acquired to aid the primary functions.

- Firm infrastructure refers to systems and assets for planning, finance, quality control and management.
- Human resources are all the activities involved in recruiting, deploying, retaining and developing people in the organisation.
- Technology development activities relate to both equipment, systems and methods of work organisation: product design and improvement of production processes and resource utilisation.
- Procurement is all activities to acquire inputs for primary activities.

The contribution of procurement

2.11 Porter's value chain model relates to the entire organisation, and adopts primarily a manufacturing perspective. We need to focus now on the specific contribution that procurement can bring, and to consider all organisations, including service firms and public sector bodies.

2.12 We commented earlier that value can be added either by cutting costs (but without loss of quality or product features), or by operational efficiency (leading to superior quality or product features at no additional cost). Ideally, we aim to achieve both of these objectives: improved output at reduced cost.

2.13 Here are some of the ways in which the procurement function can help.
- By selecting appropriate suppliers they can improve the quality of inputs, with consequent improvement in the quality of outputs.
- By effective negotiation and/or tendering they can reduce the cost of inputs.
- By effective functional management they can reduce the cost of processing purchase transactions.
- By effective dialogue with user departments they can improve specifications so that procurement needs are fulfilled more efficiently and at lower cost.
- By effective liaison with user departments and suppliers they can ensure that inputs surplus to requirements are eliminated.
- By effective inventory management they can minimise the costs of acquiring and holding stock.

2.14 To improve procurement's efforts in this area we are concerned with measuring performance. In a newly developed procurement function the initial emphasis may be on cost reduction, relating both to the cost of inputs and to the cost of running the procurement function. (The focus is on improving **efficiency**.) In a more developed procurement function, measures may be introduced for more strategic aspects of the role, such as supplier relationship management. (The focus is on improving **effectiveness**.)

2.15 Table 1.2 highlights some possible measures relating to both efficiency and effectiveness.

Table 1.2 *Efficiency and effectiveness of procurement*

MEASURES OF PROCUREMENT EFFICIENCY	MEASURES OF PROCUREMENT EFFECTIVENESS
Basic purchase price of inputs	Quality of output
Cost of placing and order	Quality of service to customers
Cost of staffing the procurement function	Achieving objectives within budget
Speed of transaction processing	Quality of supplier relationships
Use of information technology	Impact on profitability
Efficiency of organisational structure	Prompt delivery to customers
Efficiency of supplier management	

3 Value for money

Cost savings from improved performance

3.1 Buyers are naturally concerned with reducing input costs. However, this should not be taken to imply that the sole or principal function of procurement is to achieve cost reductions. On the contrary, there is a delicate balance between cost considerations and other factors which procurement professionals must be adept in managing.

3.2 The overall objective can still be stated in terms of improving profitability, but 'profit' in this sense means any benefit, and particularly long-term benefits, accruing to the organisation; and this may go far beyond short-term cost considerations. Even when we fix our attention on actual costs the modern view is that cost is a far broader concept than simple purchase price. Current thinking emphasises a **total cost of ownership** or **total acquisition cost** which includes a basket of costs not immediately apparent from the purchase price.

3.3 These ideas are neatly captured by Baily, Farmer, Jessop and Jones in the form of a 'price/cost iceberg': see Figure 1.2.

3.4 The diagram illustrates the important point that there is much more to procurement than the basic price charged by the supplier. The total costs of ownership include a wide range of other costs which must also be considered by the buyer. As the authors state, 'it is an obvious fact, yet a commonly ignored one, that a low price may lead to a high total acquisition cost'.

Figure 1.2 *The price/cost iceberg*

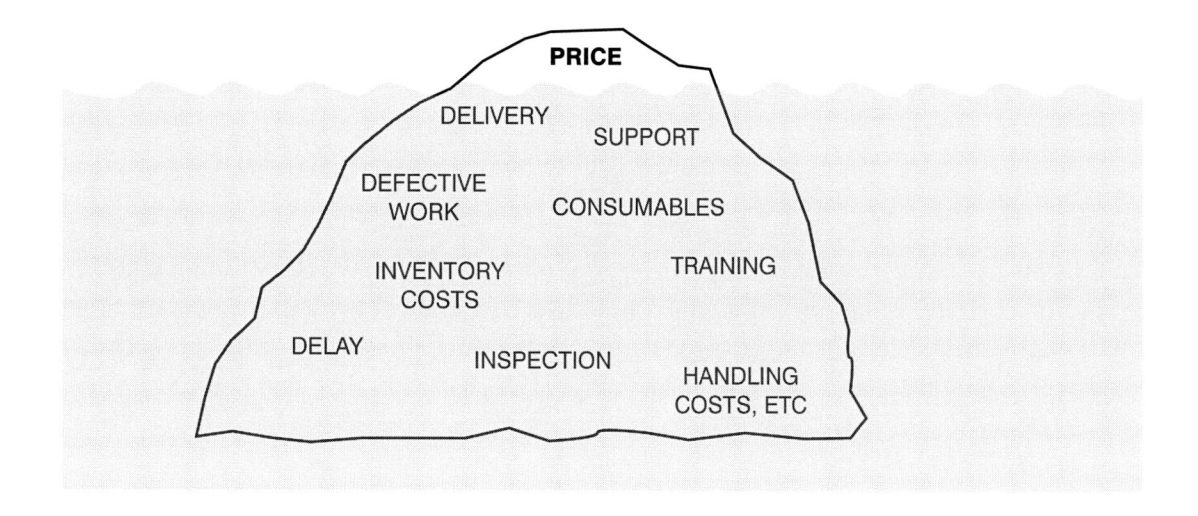

Purchase price as one element of total cost

3.5 Changing perceptions of the role of procurement have led to broader perspectives on the elements of cost that arise from procurement activities. There has been a move away from the perception that procurement is a function divided from other departments by boundary walls. That earlier perception dictated that procurement must be evaluated on its success in the activities that belonged specifically within its own remit. In other words, the success of procurement was evaluated solely on the amount paid for incoming materials.

3.6 A newer emphasis on overall corporate performance has reduced the importance of functional boundaries. Senior managers have focused on eliminating what are called **suboptimal decisions**: that is, decisions which make sense in the light of functional targets but have a damaging effect on overall performance.

3.7 This can be illustrated by very simple examples drawn from procurement.
- It would be easy for Procurement to reduce the price of incoming materials by ordering an inferior quality. However, while this might look like a success for Procurement, the increased costs elsewhere (rejects, rework, disruption to production, customer dissatisfaction etc) would outweigh any savings achieved.
- Similarly, procurement staff might be tempted to take advantage of discounts for bulk purchases, without taking account of the stockholding costs this incurs.

3.8 These examples arise from poorly designed performance measures, emphasising the performance of particular departments without regard to overall corporate performance.

3.9 What these simple examples show is that basic purchase price is just one element in the total costs that are attributable to bought out materials. Managers must take a broader view which does not focus on one particular function, but crosses functional boundaries to look at the organisation as a whole. Indeed, some would go further and argue that even boundaries between organisations in the supply chain should be disregarded in order to reduce costs for everyone.

3.10 The implications of this way of thinking are far-reaching. Instead of concentrating on minimising purchase price, buyers must focus on total acquisition cost, which includes such additional costs as those already illustrated above. Instead of operating as a closed function, separate from the rest of the organisation, buyers become part of a multi-functional team.

Cost reduction strategy

3.11 Cost reduction will be a key objective to support the financial goals of the firm (profitability, liquidity, return on capital invested and so on), even in the public sector (with goals such as value for money service provision and efficiency targets). It will be the cornerstone of business strategies based on cost leadership.

3.12 Cost strategies are about knowing what the costs really are and then looking at how to reduce them. In other words, we must apply effective cost analysis, with a particular focus on total cost of ownership or total acquisition costs: purchase price plus delivery, support, consumables, staff training, inventory and handling costs, inspection, maintenance and repair, and so on, over the useful life of the asset. Then we are in a position to look at eliminating waste, negotiating on price and so on.

3.13 At a strategic level, supply chain management may secure cost reductions through measures such as the following.

- **Restructuring**: delayering, downsizing or horizontalising procurement structures, to minimise labour and overhead costs and maximise process efficiencies (less duplication of effort, fewer managerial and co-ordinatory mechanisms and so on)
- **Centralising procurement** (to take advantage of aggregated orders and bargaining leverage) or devolving procurement (to reduce transport and storage costs)
- **Process engineering or re-engineering**, to streamline and integrate processes, eliminating unnecessary activities and process inefficiencies
- **Outsourcing or off-shoring** non-core competencies: where value can be obtained at less cost, the organisation can dispose of assets, and internal resources can be more efficiently focused
- **Developing supplier relationships for cost and price advantages** (whether by using competitive leverage to secure low prices or by developing collaboration to reduce sourcing and transaction costs, encourage mutual cost reduction and so on)
- **Applying ICT** and automation technologies to streamline processes (eg the use of e-procurement tools); increase productivity and reduce labour costs; reduce overheads (eg by 'virtual' teamworking); secure competitive pricing (eg through internet access to global supply markets, or the use of e-auctions); support more efficient planning and decision-making (via computerised planning models), and so on.

Obtaining value for money

3.14 There is frequently a trade-off between cost objectives and objectives relating to quality, service and delivery. This has led to the recognition that cost/price and 'value' are not the same thing. 'Value for money' is an important strategic objective, particularly in the public and non-profit sector. It may be defined as 'the optimum combination of whole life cost and the quality necessary to meet the customer's requirement'.

3.15 A number of procurement techniques can be used to obtain value for money.

- **The use of value analysis** (and/or value engineering of new products and processes), in order to eliminate non-essential features. This means looking critically at all the elements that make up a product or service and investigating whether they are really necessary, whether they could be done more efficiently or cheaply etc
- **Consolidation of demand** (eg by variety reduction, aggregating orders or using buying consortia to negotiate reduced prices)
- **Centralised negotiation** of contracts and prices
- **Proactive sourcing**: challenging preferred supplier complacency to ensure competitive value. (Supply contracts may contain provision for year-on-year price reductions, for example, as an incentive to efficiency improvements.)
- Buying complete subassemblies rather than components
- Encouraging standardisation to reduce costs of spares and maintenance
- Adopting whole life costing methodologies (rather than focusing on purchase price)
- Eliminating or reducing inventory (and therefore storage, holding, deterioration and obsolescence costs)
- Using e-procurement for process efficiencies
- Global procurement (to take advantage of low-cost country production)

4 Products and services

Why services are different

4.1 So far, when we have discussed the sourcing requirements of organisations, we have lumped together products and services. But the fact is that, in many ways, they are not the same.

4.2 A service may be defined as 'any activity or benefit that one party can offer to another that is essentially intangible and does not result in ownership of anything' (Kotler). Some obvious examples include call-centre, cleaning, transport and logistics, and IT services: something is 'done for you', but there is no transfer of ownership of anything as part of the service transaction. (It is also worth remembering that some form of service is part of the 'bundle of benefits' you acquire when you purchase materials and goods: sales service, customer service, delivery, after-sales care, warranties and so on.)

4.3 Services (and service elements) present buyers with problems additional to those that arise in purchasing materials or manufactured goods, when it comes to specifying requirements.

- Goods are tangible: they can be inspected, measured, weighed and tested to check quality and compliance with specification. Services are *intangible*: specifying service levels – and subsequently checking whether or how far they have been achieved – is therefore fraught with difficulty. As Steve Kirby notes: 'How clean is clean? How long should it take to repair a computer? What is the definition of a well-cooked meal?' This is an aspect of the **right quality** in the purchase of services.
- Goods emerging from a manufacturing process generally have a high degree of uniformity, which also simplifies their evaluation. Services are *variable*: every separate instance of service provision is unique, because the personnel and circumstances are different. It is hard to standardise requirements. This is another aspect of the **right quality**.
- Goods can be produced, purchased and stored in advance of need, for later consumption. Services are *inseparable* and *perishable*, provided in 'real time': they can't be provided first and consumed later. Transport, accommodation and catering services, for example, are only relevant when they are needed. Specifications therefore need to include the time of provision, so that the supplier can schedule provision accordingly. This is an aspect of the **right time**.
- Goods can often be used anywhere, once purchased. Many services can only be performed in particular locations (eg accommodation provided at a hotel premises, cleaning provided at the buyer's offices). The service specification may therefore need to include explicit understandings about where the service is to be provided, the access required and related issues (such as confidentiality, if suppliers are working on the buyers' premises). This is an aspect of the **right place**.
- The exact purpose for which a tangible good is used will usually be known, and its suitability can therefore be assessed objectively. It is harder to assess the many factors involved in providing a service: what weight should be placed on the friendliness or smart appearance of the supplier's staff, say, compared with the efficiency with which they get the job done? This is another aspect of the **right quality**.
- Goods are usually purchased for more or less immediate use, such as incorporation in a larger product, or onward sale. A service may be purchased for a long period, during which requirements may change from the original specification. This is another aspect of the **right time**.

Service level agreements

4.4 Service level agreements (SLAs) are formal statements of performance requirements, specifying the exact nature and level of service to be provided by a service supplier, as part of a service specification. The purpose of a service level specification and agreement is to define the customer's service level needs and secure the commitment of the supplier to meeting those needs: this can then be used as a yardstick against which to measure the supplier's subsequent performance, conformance (meeting standards) and compliance (fulfilling agreed terms).

4.5 The main objective of an SLA is to quantify (state in specific, measurable terms) the minimum quality of service which will meet the customer's business needs, as a basis for the monitoring and maintenance of service levels.

4.6 The main *benefits* of effective SLAs, as summarised by Lysons & Farrington, are as follows.

- The clear identification of customers and providers, in relation to specific services
- The focusing of attention on what services actually involve and achieve
- Identification of the real service requirements of the customer, and potential for costs to be reduced by cutting services or levels of service that (a) are unnecessary and (b) do not add value
- Better customer awareness of what services they receive, what they are entitled to expect, and what additional services or levels of service a provider can offer
- Better customer awareness of what a service or level of service costs, for realistic cost-benefit evaluation
- Support for the ongoing monitoring and periodic review of services and service levels
- Support for problem solving and improvement planning, by facilitating customers in reporting failure to meet service levels
- The fostering of better understanding and trust between providers and customers

4.7 Lysons & Farrington also cite the following main reasons why SLAs *fail to achieve* their objectives.

- Lack of commitment by providers and/or customers
- Lack of consultation with user departments and other stakeholders, as to the services and levels of service actually required
- Inadequate support structure (eg no manager responsible for the SLA, no cross-functional project team to implement the SLA, no service level review meetings)
- Overloading of staff with extra work involved in SLAs (eg additional monitoring and reporting tasks)
- Overly detailed SLAs, which become burdensome to monitor
- Insufficiently detailed or specific SLAs, which allow problems to 'slip through the cracks'
- Inadequate staff training in the purpose and implementation of SLAs.

4.8 Note our emphasis on ascertaining what services and levels of service are actually required, and on examining what they actually achieve and whether they add value. It is important not to *over-specify* requirements – for services as for goods. Specifying unnecessarily high standards or frequency of service, tight response times or grade of staff adds cost without necessarily adding value. (This is a point particularly worth making in a time of recession – and worth looking out for in exam situations, where purchasers may well be under cost pressures.)

Contents of a service level agreement

4.9 The basic elements of an SLA are as follows.

- What services are included (and not included, or included only on request and at additional cost)
- Standards or levels of service (such as response times, speed and attributes of quality service)
- The allocation of responsibility for activities, risks and costs
- How services and service levels will be monitored and reviewed, what measures of evaluation will be used, and how problems (if any) will be addressed
- How complaints and disputes will be managed
- When and how the agreement will be reviewed and revised. (Service specifications may need to change as requirements or circumstances change.)

4.10 Of course, these elements will be adapted to the specific nature of the service contract. As an example, suppose a company decides to hire external suppliers to provide office cleaning services. The basic service level issues for agreement will include the following.

- How often is the service to be provided? **(Right time)**
- During what hours will the service be carried out, and will there be any disruption to office activities? **(Right time)**
- How many staff (and, if relevant, with what skills, qualifications or experience levels) will be involved in providing the service? **(Right quality)**
- How far will the service extend (eg does it include cleaning of computer monitors and desktop areas? Does it exclude washing up left in the staff kitchen?) **(Right place and right quality)**
- Does the service include special tasks caused by fault of the buyer's staff (eg wiping up spillages)? If so, how will the costs be attributed or shared? **(Right quality and right price)**
- What speed of response is expected from the supplier when the customer makes a non-routine service request? What speed of response is expected for a request categorised as 'urgent', and what extra costs might this incur? **(Right time)**
- How will cleaners report completion of their work and any issues or problems that arose? How will customers monitor and feed back their evaluation of the work? How will customer complaints be dealt with? **(Right quality)**
- What rates will the supplier pay its staff? (If these appear to be below average, there may be an ethical issue – as well as a potential impact on the quality of service likely to be delivered.) **(Right quality)**

Chapter summary

- Procurement is a professional discipline. Its objectives are to achieve the five rights: inputs of the right quality, delivered in the right quantity, to the right place, at the right time for the right price.
- Porter's value chain model shows how procurement (and other support activities) can add value across all the firm's primary activities.
- The basic purchase price is only one element in the total cost of a procurement.
- Services have characteristics that differentiate them from tangible products. Even so, the five rights can still be applied to procurement of services.

Self-test questions

Numbers in brackets refer to paragraphs where you can check your answers

1. List the five rights of procurement. (Table 1.1)
2. What is meant by 'good practice' in procurement? (1.6)
3. Sketch Porter's value chain model. (Figure 1.1)
4. In what ways can Procurement help to obtain improved output at reduced cost? (2.13)
5. List elements of total cost other than the basic purchase price. (Figure 1.2)
6. List strategic methods by which cost reductions can be achieved. (3.13)
7. List factors that differentiate services from tangible products. (4.3)
8. What are the main benefits of service level agreements? (4.6)

CHAPTER 2

The Right Price

Assessment criteria and indicative content

1.2 Analyse techniques to secure competitive pricing
- Using competition to obtain quotations on prices
- Comparing prices quoted to historical data
- Suppliers' approaches to pricing
- The link between costs and prices
- Negotiating improved prices
- Securing competitive pricing through competition or collaboration with suppliers
- Measuring achieved savings

2.3 Assess approaches to the sourcing of supplies
- Inviting quotations and tenders
- Assessing quotations and tenders

Section headings

1. What is the right price?
2. Suppliers' approaches to pricing
3. The link between costs and prices
4. Using competition to obtain quotations
5. Measuring achieved savings

Introduction

There is a temptation for buyers to think of the 'right' price simply as the lowest price – especially if the procurement function's performance is judged on the basis of cost control or cost reductions. But, as we will see, this is not always the case. The aim of purchasers will be to secure the lowest price consistent with achieving all the other 'rights', and there is frequently a trade-off involved. You can probably get your goods faster, but at a higher price. You can probably get your goods cheaper, but at a lower quality. If you buy in higher quantities, you may get a bulk discount on the price – but will also incur higher costs of holding stock.

In this chapter, we explore these various trade-offs in deciding on the 'right' price. We also look at the information and analysis required to decide on what is a 'fair' or 'reasonable' price for a supplier to charge, taking into account what the market will accept, what pricing strategies the supplier is using – and the supplier's need to make a profit. This also leads us into the complex area of 'costs', because the supplier will need to charge a price that at least covers its costs and provides for some profit. If a buyer knows what a supplier's costs are, he can judge whether the price is reasonable – and how far it may be negotiable.

1 What is the right price?

1.1 Price may be defined as 'the value of a commodity or service measured in terms of the standard monetary unit' (Lysons & Farrington). In other words, price is what a supplier charges for goods or services – and if two suppliers quote different prices, a purchaser can readily compare the relative value offered by each.

1.2 So what does it mean to buy at the 'right' price? The purchasing firm will be seeking to make a profit. It may also be seeking specifically to control or reduce its costs – and may expect the procurement function to play a major part in this by reducing the cost of obtaining materials, goods and services. So the 'right' price may simply be the lowest price available.

1.3 However, remember that we have already established the need to buy goods of the right quality, in the right quantity, at the right time, delivered to the right place. The 'right' price will therefore be the best or lowest price available, consistent with ensuring the right quality, quantity, timing and delivery. In other words, what the purchaser is after is **value for money** – not just a 'cheap' price.

1.4 Obtaining value for money means not paying too much for the total package of value (quality and service) you are getting. It also, perhaps more surprisingly, means not paying too little: a very low price may reflect a supplier's desire to win your business – but it may also result in corner cutting on quality somewhere along the line, because, as they say, 'if you pay peanuts, you get monkeys'!

1.5 In fact, there are a number of other requirements for the 'right price', seen from the supplier's point of view as well as from the buyer's point of view.

Sales price

1.6 The 'right price' for the supplier or seller to charge (the right sales price) will be:
- A price which 'the market will bear': that is, a price that the market or a particular buyer will be willing to pay
- A price which allows the seller to win business, in competition with other suppliers (according to how badly it needs the business, and the prices being charged by its competitors)
- A price which allows the seller at least to cover its costs, and ideally to make a healthy profit which will allow it to survive in business and to invest in growth.

Procurement price

1.7 The 'right price' for the buyer to pay (the right procurement price) will be:
- A price which the purchaser can afford: allowing it to control its costs of production and make a profit on sale of its own goods or services
- A price which appears fair and reasonable, or represents value for money, for the total package of benefits being purchased
- A price which gives the purchaser a cost or quality advantage over its competitors, enabling it to compete more effectively in its own market
- A price which reflects sound procurement practices: requiring suppliers to price competitively; negotiating skilfully; recognising the difference between strategic/critical and non-critical/routine purchases; and so on.

How buyers obtain a price

1.8 There are various methods by which suppliers can communicate prices to buyers, or by which buyers can ascertain the price of the goods they are interested in.

- Suppliers may have a *standard price list*, available in printed form, or posted online, or published within a catalogue. This is common with standard articles and industrial components. Discounts on 'list price' are often available for bulk purchase, or for prompt or early payment; to secure the business of an attractive or high-status client; or to stimulate demand (eg 'off-season' discounts, promotional discounts and special offers).
- Prices may be *quoted on request*: based on an internal price list (not seen by buyers) or on specially prepared estimates for the proposed contract. Quotations may be included in a sealed bid or tender by the supplier, as part of a competitive bidding process.
- Prices may be arrived at through *negotiation* between the supplier and the buyer.
- Prices may be determined by *competition*, in an auction (where buyers bid for goods offered for sale, and the highest bid wins) or reverse auction (where suppliers bid to supply goods advertised as wanted, and the lowest bid wins).
- Prices may be determined by the *market* eg for commodities and other materials which are traded in market exchanges: 'market prices' are published on the exchange, and in the national press and trade journals.

1.9 The more specialised or customised the buyer's requirement, the less likely there is to be a 'standard' price or price list, and prices are more likely to be estimated and negotiated by buyer and supplier on the basis of the requirement.

Price analysis

1.10 When considering the prices quoted by a supplier, or offered in negotiation, there are two basic approaches that a buyer can use to decide whether 'the price is right'.

- Price analysis
- Cost analysis.

1.11 *Price analysis* simply seeks to determine if the price offered is a fair and appropriate price for the goods. The 'right' price in this sense may be one which is advantageous or reasonable compared to: the prices offered by other suppliers (competitive tenders or quotations); the prices previously paid by the buyer for the same goods or services; the market or 'going' rate; and/or the price of any alternative or substitute goods.

1.12 Does this mean that if you receive several quotations, you can simply discard the offers with prices above the norm and accept prices below the norm? Not necessarily.

- Low prices may be the result of a supplier's needing to secure work to maintain production and sales: the supplier may only seek to cover its essential costs (or direct costs, a concept which we will discuss later in the chapter), and accept less in the way of contribution to covering its overheads (or indirect costs) and making a profit. In other words, it will accept a lower profit margin. This represents good value to a buyer – but it may still be worth asking why the supplier is currently short of work. (Is it due to economic downturn or seasonal fluctuations, which may affect anyone – or due to having lost other customers through poor quality work?)
- On the other hand, low prices may be the result of a supplier's being highly profitable, and therefore being able to afford to lower its prices in response to negotiation – or to secure the

business of a new or lucrative client. This again may represent good value to a buyer – but he should also be aware that such discounted (or 'introductory offer') prices may not always be available. Both parties will want to be clear that special offers cannot be made the basis for standard prices.
- Low prices may also be quoted by mistake (eg a mistake in estimating costs)! Ethical buyers will not take advantage of such scenarios: if the quoted price is well below the average, a buyer should query it and allow the supplier to adjust the quote or withdraw the offer. Forcing a supplier to stand by a price at which it could only fulfil the order at a loss may lead to supplier failure and broken supplier relationships – which may, in the long run, be more expensive than taking the ethical path.
- Unusually high prices may be quoted if the supplier's order book is already full (ie it does not need the business, unless super-normal profit can be earned). The supplier is not necessarily 'more expensive' than competitors, and may offer a competitive quote for subsequent orders.
- Higher prices may also reflect a better specification or a higher level of service, and this should be taken into account. Low price is not the only consideration for buyers: the 'best value' purchase will balance quality, delivery and cost.

1.13 We will look at some key concepts and tools for price analysis in Section 2 of this chapter.

Cost analysis

1.14 *Cost analysis* is a more specialised technique, often used to support price negotiations where the supplier justifies its price by the need to cover its costs (cost-based pricing, which we will explain further below). Cost analysis looks specifically at how the quoted price relates to the supplier's cost of production. Suppliers may be asked to include cost breakdowns with their price quotations, so that:

- Differences between the supplier's cost breakdown and the buyer's own analysis or estimate of the supplier's costs can be examined to arrive at an agreed cost figure
- Buyers can identify when suppliers are claiming higher-than-average or unjustifiable profit margins
- Buyers can calculate a target price or price range for use in negotiation (based on suppliers covering their costs plus a reasonable profit margin).

1.15 Not all suppliers will be willing to share their detailed cost information with buyers (an approach called **cost transparency**). However, if they can be persuaded to do so – often, as part of a trusting buyer-supplier relationship – there are several benefits to cost analysis. It can keep prices realistic (ie no unreasonably large profit margins), in the absence of competition – for example, where there is a preferred supplier. It focuses attention on what costs ought to be involved in producing the goods or services, which acts as an incentive for cost control and reduction, and which may in turn lead to cost savings passed on to the buyer.

1.16 We will look at some key concepts and tools for cost analysis in Section 3 of this chapter.

Comparing prices quoted to historical data

1.17 Historical prices are previously proposed prices and validated contract prices that were paid for the same or similar items in the past. The purchase associated with a particular price may have been made by our own branch of the organisation or another branch with similar requirements. The prior price used for comparison must be validated and reasonably current in order to be used for comparison.

1.18 Historical data can provide a guide as to trends in the pricing of items and, subject to the points detailed below, can provide valuable information to the purchaser. One key area when a knowledge of historical prices is important is during negotiations with suppliers. In this situation a detailed background knowledge can help the buyer to convince a supplier that he has carried out thorough and relevant research prior to the negotiation.

1.19 Table 2.1 sets out some points to consider in relation to historical prices.

Table 2.1 *Historical prices*

CONSIDERATION	EXPLANATION
Has the product been purchased before?	The purchase may have been made by our own branch or by another.
What was the historical price?	We can obtain price information from purchase files, computer data files, or manual inventory item records.
Was the historical price fair and reasonable?	For a historical price to be useful in determining the reasonableness of an offered price, we must know that the historical price was fair and reasonable. It is not uncommon to review an item's purchase history and find that that there has been a significant time lapse between the last acquisition and the present one.
Is the comparison valid?	For the comparison to be valid, we must be able to identify and consider any market differences that might significantly affect contract price.
Was the price adjusted?	The prior price must be adjusted to account for materially differing terms and conditions, quantities and market and economic factors. The analysis must also account for minor modifications.
Discount arrangements	Commercial sales typically include discounts for different types of customers. Discount amounts typically depend on the product and the marketing strategy of the firm. Common factors affecting discounts include services provided by the seller (eg wholesale and retail sales) and the importance of the sale (eg quantity purchased or the relationship to other sales).
Rebate arrangements	Rebates are often offered to customers based on the customer's total purchases over a specific period of time.
Differences in the contracting situation	Our contracting situation may be different from the situation in the commercial market. For example, the supplier may provide services to commercial customers that are not required by, say, local authorities. If the local authority is receiving less, you should expect to pay less. It is important to identify these differences and determine what impact, if any, they have on the price of the item.

Negotiating improved prices

1.20 Negotiation is defined by Dobler *et al*, in the procurement context, as: 'A process of planning, reviewing and analysing used by a buyer and a seller to reach acceptable agreements or compromises [which] include all aspects of the business transaction, not just price'.

1.21 The detail of price negotiation is beyond the scope of the syllabus. It is worth noting, however, that there are two basic approaches to price negotiation.

- *Distributive bargaining* involves the distribution of limited resources, or 'dividing up a fixed pie'. One party's gain can only come at the expense of the other party: this is sometimes called a zero-sum game, or a win-lose outcome. If the buyer pushes the price down, for example, the supplier's profit margin will be eroded.

- *Integrative bargaining* involves collaborative problem-solving to increase the options available (or 'expanding the pie'), with the aim of exploring possibilities for both parties to find a mutually satisfying or win-win solution. This may also be called 'added value negotiating' (AVN): the aim is to add value to the deal, rather than extracting value from or conceding value to the other party.

1.22 The foundation for win-win or integrative approaches in supply negotiations is the belief that co-operation along the supply chain can lead to elimination of waste and performance improvements, benefiting all parties. A buyer who focuses exclusively on one objective – say, gaining a 5% price reduction – may miss opportunities to widen the discussion fruitfully. For example, by co-operating with the supplier in improved quality assurance measures, the costs of quality may fall for both parties: this may be enough in itself to achieve the desired improvement in profits, without squeezing the supplier's margins.

1.23 We now go on to explore the underlying factors in suppliers' pricing decisions.

2 Suppliers' approaches to pricing

Factors in suppliers' pricing decisions

2.1 A wide range of factors may be taken into account by suppliers when setting the 'right price' for their business interests, and any given pricing decision will be a combination of factors, both internal and external: Table 2.2.

Table 2.2 *Factors in pricing decisions*

EXTERNAL FACTORS IN SUPPLIER PRICING DECISIONS	INTERNAL FACTORS IN SUPPLIER PRICING DECISIONS
Prices charged by competitors: the need to stay competitive to win business – while avoiding potentially damaging price wars	Costs of production and sales, which must be matched by sales revenue in order to earn profits
Extent of competition (market structure): with little competition, the supplier can charge what he likes; with lots of undifferentiated competition, 'the market' decides the price	How badly the supplier needs the business at a particular time (eg to cover fixed costs, cover the costs of research and development of a new product, gain cashflow, reassure shareholders)
The nature of competition in the market, which may (or may not) be based on price	Risk management: eg making provision in the price to cover unforeseen costs or changes
Market conditions: levels of demand and supply, dictating the price that the market will bear. If demand exceeds supply, prices rise; if supply exceeds demand, prices fall.	How attractive a particular customer is to the supplier: pricing low to win/retain good customers, or high to penalise unattractive (eg late-paying, low-volume) customers
Customer perceptions of value: different perceptions of value for money; willingness to pay a premium for 'quality' and so on	Financial position and product portfolio, which may (or may not) allow the supplier to accept occasional losses to secure business
Price elasticity of demand: the extent to which market demand rises or falls with changes in price	Where the product is in its 'lifecycle': eg new products need higher prices to cover the costs of research and development.
What a particular (desirable, powerful) customer is prepared to pay	Shareholders' expectations and managerial objectives in regard to profit margins
Environmental factors affecting the cost of raw materials (eg weather, disrupted supply, shortage of raw materials)	The strategic objectives of the organisation: positioning as a 'value for money' or 'premium' provider; increasing market share (by competitive pricing); and so on.
Environmental factors affecting demand and affordability: eg economic recession reducing spending; government regulators	

2.2 Most of these points should be logical and self-explanatory. We'll just look at some of the major concepts introduced in the table, briefly.

Pricing strategies

2.3 Lysons & Farrington offer the following summary of pricing strategies or models, based on either (a) costs or (b) market factors: Figure 2.1.

Figure 2.1 *Pricing models*

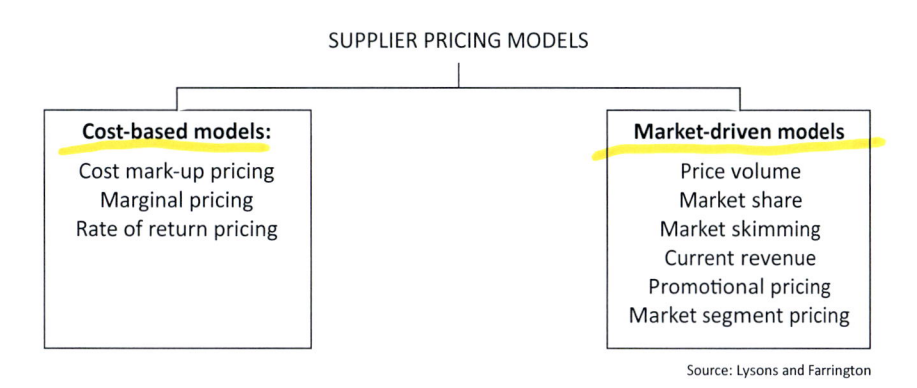

```
                    SUPPLIER PRICING MODELS
                              |
              ┌───────────────┴───────────────┐
    Cost-based models:                Market-driven models
    Cost mark-up pricing              Price volume
    Marginal pricing                  Market share
    Rate of return pricing            Market skimming
                                      Current revenue
                                      Promotional pricing
                                      Market segment pricing
```

Source: Lysons and Farrington

2.4 We will look at cost-based models a bit later, when we have examined suppliers' costs in more detail. Essentially, cost-based pricing seeks to cover costs (which may be calculated in various ways) and allow for an extra sum to secure a reasonable profit.

2.5 The market-driven models mentioned by Lysons & Farrington can be explained briefly as follows.

- **Price volume**: the supplier uses cost-volume-profit (or breakeven) analysis to determine a volume of production which will be most economical (spreading overhead costs over a larger number of units), and will allow him to offer quantity discounts to buyers, which will in turn increase sales.
- **Market share pricing** (or **penetration pricing**): the supplier sets low introductory prices that will win customers and/or discourage or eliminate competition (because of the low profit margins available in the market). The aim may be (a) to stimulate the growth of a market, by getting people to try a new product or (b) to increase the supplier's share of the market (a strategy of 'market penetration'). As the supplier's market share and sales volume increase, it is able to produce more, at a lower cost per unit, and therefore reap better profits. It may be able to raise prices later (taking advantage of customer loyalty and discouraged competition) and still dominate the market. This strategy is most successful in the following circumstances.
  - Unit costs of production fall with increased output volume
  - The market is relatively price sensitive, so that low prices will attract more sales
  - The supplier is able to reduce his costs in a way that competitors are not able to emulate (a strategy of 'cost leadership').
- **Market skimming**: the supplier sets a *high* introductory price, to attract buyers who (a) have a strong desire to get the product early (while it is innovative and may present a competitive advantage for them); and (b) can afford it. In other words, the supplier maximises its short-term profits early on ('skims the cream off the top'), gradually reducing prices over time to attract further 'layers' of buyers, who are more price sensitive. This also enables the supplier to recoup some of the costs of research and development, and the costs of marketing a new product. (In a consumer market, for example, you might think about the introduction of an

innovative product like the original Apple iPhone.) A skimming strategy is most successful when:
- Competitors are not able to increase capacity (supply), so that early adopters have to pay a premium price to gain access to the product
- The market is relatively price inelastic, owing to the newness and scarcity of the product (in the early stage of its 'product lifecycle')
- The high price is perceived as justified on grounds of quality or advantage.

- **Current revenue pricing** (or **contribution pricing**): the supplier aims to cover his operating costs, rather than earning profits. It may accept an order at or below cost because, without the order, the lack of demand will necessitate shutting down part of its production, incurring lay-off costs, shut-down and re-start costs and so on.
- **Promotional pricing**: the supplier offers a discount for a specific, limited period, in order to boost short-term sales. (This is common in consumer market 'sales promotions', but the technique may also be used in 'trade promotions'.)
- **Market segment pricing** (also called **differential pricing** or **price discrimination**): the supplier sets different prices for different market segments, depending on the price they will bear – and the different value received by different customers. In consumer markets, you can see this in the difference between 'peak' and 'off-peak' travel or telephone charges. A supplier may offer lower prices to overseas buyers, however, or may offer 'deluxe/professional' and 'standard/economy' versions of its products at different prices to different users: think about computer software, for example.
- **Competition pricing** (or **dynamic pricing**): the supplier 'bids' competitively to win a contract, eg in a reverse auction, by setting the highest price that is lower than competitors' prices.

2.6 A further strategy, common in consumer markets, is known as **psychological pricing**, in which the supplier recognises the psychological element in price perception and sensitivity. Prices are perceived in different ways by customers, according to their context and how they are communicated. For example:

- Prices may be set according to what customers expect to pay for goods of a certain quality. (A well-known beer brand once marketed itself as 'Reassuringly expensive'.) Higher prices are often associated with 'premium' (quality) or high-status products.
- In retail selling, the concept of a 'quantum point' is often referred to. When the price of an item is increased from $90 to $99, customers may not be price sensitive – but if it is increased from $99 to $101, a fall in sales may occur, because a certain point ($100) has been passed, beyond which customers perceive the price as too expensive.
- Similarly, 'odd number pricing' is used because $99 is perceived as significantly better value than $100.
- Product ranges often deliberately include a very high priced item, next to which the second-highest-priced article 'looks' like good value: still high quality, but not the most expensive – and therefore a 'bargain'.

2.7 The following is a brief comparison of the arguments for skimming and penetration strategies: Table 2.3.

Table 2.3 *Arguments for skimming and penetration pricing*

MARKET SKIMMING	MARKET PENETRATION
Offsets high costs of development with early positive cashflow	Designed to induce customer trial, potentially leading to brand loyalty
Capitalises on customer willingness to pay premium prices for new or differentiated products (eg 'green' or ethical procurement)	Encourages demand, potentially supporting economies of scale in production and marketing
Higher price may create quality perception	Lower price may create value perception
Offers flexibility to lower or discount prices later, to attract next layers of market	Offers flexibility to raise or differentiate prices later, once loyalty is achieved

Factors in buyers' decisions on price

2.8 So far, we have talked about how suppliers go about deciding what prices to charge. However, we must also mention how buyers go about deciding what prices to accept. Here are some of the factors in such a decision.

- The buying organisation's relative bargaining power in the market and relationship. (A monopoly supplier may have power to set prices as it wishes – but if a buyer represents a large proportion of a supplier's business, he will be in a strong position to negotiate favourable prices.)
- The number of suppliers in the market and the possibility of substitute products (enabling the buyer to exploit competition to force prices down)
- The type of purchase. For non-critical or routine products, for example, a buyer will want to secure best price by competitive procurement, while for critical or strategic products, he may pay more for service and security of supply.
- The prices paid by competitors (if this information is available), so that the buyer keeps his materials costs competitive
- The total package of benefits offered for the price, and whether 'value' is better at a higher price (given the need for quality, delivery, supplier relationship and so on)
- What the buyer can afford, given the quantities likely to be involved over a given period
- What is a 'reasonable' price, based on price analysis
- What is a 'fair' (ethical and sustainable) price from the buyer's and supplier's point of view.

2.9 The decision on what is a reasonable price, and what is a fair price, depends on the supplier's costs and profit aspirations. So let's now look at the major price-related issues of cost and profit.

3 The link between costs and prices

3.1 It may seem like an obvious point, but it is important to distinguish clearly between 'price' and 'cost' – especially when reading exam questions! Price, as we have seen, is what a seller charges for a package of benefits offered to a buyer. Cost is what the buying organisation pays to acquire and utilise the goods purchased: as we have seen, this may be much more than just the purchase price paid to the seller. Moreover, the seller also has costs: the finance and resources it expends in producing and providing goods and services. And a buyer cannot routinely expect the (purchase) price of goods to be the same as their cost (of production) – otherwise, the supplier would not make a profit, and would be unlikely to survive.

3.2 It is important for purchasers to understand that suppliers are entitled to make a profit. That is, they are entitled to set or quote prices on goods which allow them to cover their costs and make a reasonable 'profit margin' for their owners, or to reinvest in the business. This is called **cost-based pricing**.

Understanding the supplier's cost base

3.3 There are three major areas in which a manufacturing business incurs costs. (If an exam question refers to different 'types' of cost that may affect pricing, or different 'components' of a supplier's costs, this is probably what the question is referring to – although you might also choose to discuss 'direct and indirect' or 'fixed and variable' costs, which we will mention a bit later.)

- *Raw materials* (and/or components, subassemblies and consumables): the 'inputs' to the manufacturing process
- *Labour*: the wages or salaries of workers employed by the organisation
- *Overheads*: expenditure which cannot be directly identified with the output of any particular production item, but is associated with keeping business processes up and running. Overheads may be sub-divided into production or manufacturing overheads (eg electricity, maintenance and set-up costs); administration overheads (eg office expenses and management costs); and selling/distribution overheads (eg marketing, advertising and sales force costs, and storage, transport and logistics costs). *Marketing* and *logistics* may be considered as separate areas of cost.

3.4 It is worth noting that *profit* (or profit margin) is not a cost – although, along with costs, it is a component in price, or in the supplier's pricing decision. Successive Senior Examiners' reports have complained of this mark-losing misconception: beware the pitfall.

3.5 Of course, these same cost components will apply to the *purchasing* organisation as well as to the supplier. The buyer may need to analyse the costs of his or her own organisation, in order to ascertain how profitably it is selling its own products – and how the procurement function can contribute to profitability by reducing the cost of materials for the organisation.

Direct and indirect costs

3.6 One common way of classifying costs is to distinguish between direct and indirect costs.

- *Direct costs*: costs which can be identified with a specific saleable unit of output. So, for example, the direct costs of producing the textbook you are reading include: direct materials (such as paper, ink and glue); and direct labour (wages paid to employees working on the production of the book).
- *Indirect costs* (or *overheads*): expenditure on labour, materials or other items which cannot be identified with a specific saleable unit of output. For example, the indirect materials costs of this book might include the oil used to lubricate the printing press; and indirect labour costs might include the salaries of the shift supervisor and sales staff. (These costs contribute to other jobs performed by the printing press – not just this one.) Such costs are often classified as production overheads, administration overheads and selling/distribution overheads.

3.7 We can therefore build up an overall picture of a supplier's costs as follows: Figure 2.2.

Figure 2.2 *Suppliers' costs*

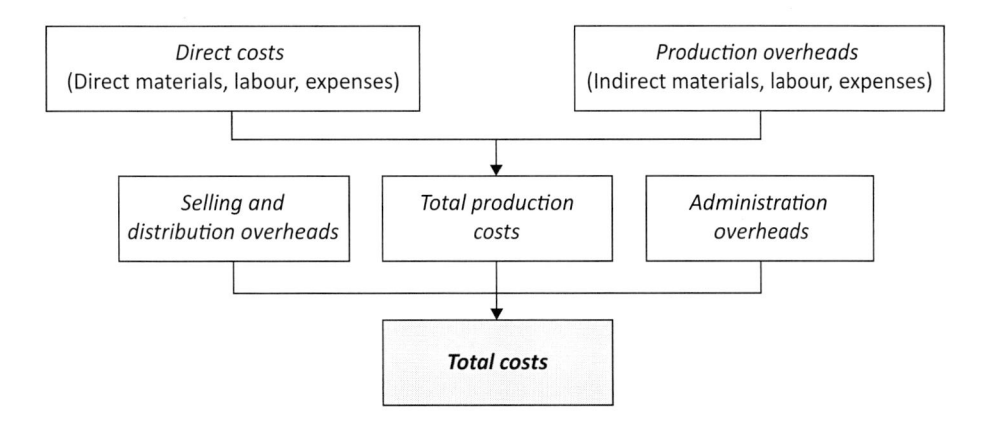

```
┌─────────────────────────┐      ┌──────────────────────────────┐
│      Direct costs       │      │     Production overheads     │
│(Direct materials,       │      │(Indirect materials,          │
│ labour, expenses)       │      │ labour, expenses)            │
└───────────┬─────────────┘      └──────────────┬───────────────┘
            │                                   │
            └─────────────┬─────────────────────┘
                          ▼
┌─────────────────┐  ┌─────────────────┐  ┌─────────────────┐
│   Selling and   │  │ Total production│  │  Administration │
│   distribution  │  │      costs      │  │    overheads    │
│    overheads    │  │                 │  │                 │
└────────┬────────┘  └────────┬────────┘  └────────┬────────┘
         │                    │                    │
         └────────────────────┼────────────────────┘
                              ▼
                     ┌─────────────────┐
                     │   Total costs   │
                     └─────────────────┘
```

Fixed and variable costs

3.8 **Cost behaviour** is the way in which the costs of output are affected by fluctuations in the level of activity: the volume of production, say, or the level of sales.

- Some costs do not vary at all as the volume of sales or production increases. If an organisation is paying rent on a factory, or paying employees a salary (not based on output), it will have to pay the same amount for a given period, whether the factory is operating or not, and however much it is producing. This type of cost is called a *fixed* cost.
- Some costs vary as the volume of sales or production increases. If an organisation uses raw materials to produce widgets, say, at a cost of $0.40 per widget, production of 10,000 widgets costs it $4,000 – but production of 20,000 widgets costs it $8,000. This type of cost is called a *variable* cost.

3.9 Fixed and variable costs are illustrated in Figure 2.3.

Figure 2.3 *Fixed and variable costs*

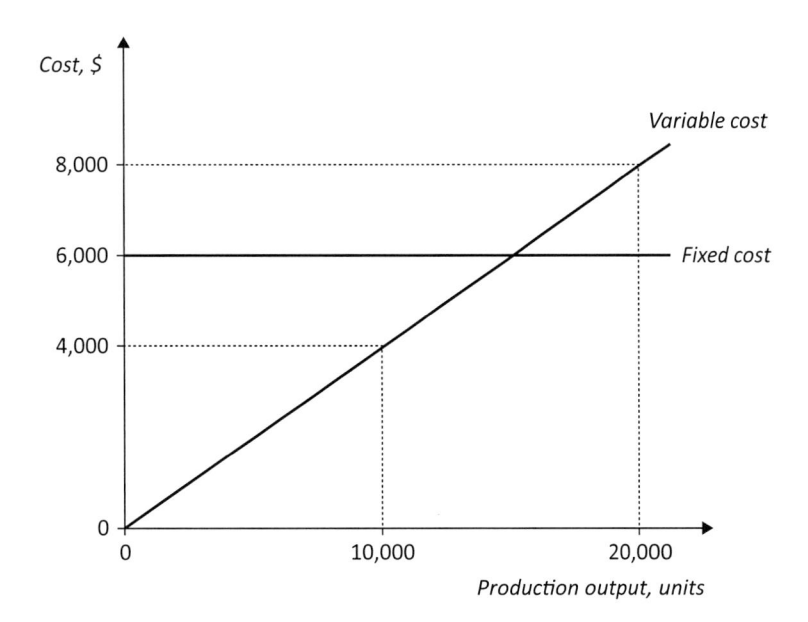

3.10 The way in which costs behave as production output changes is a key element in the way prices are set by suppliers. The supplier's sales force will always be seeking to generate at least enough business to cover fixed costs: the costs incurred by the business whether they produce anything or not. If the cost structure of the supplier includes a high proportion of fixed costs, there will be strong pressure to achieve high sales volume – and this may result in competitive, incentive-level pricing.

3.11 **Cost-based pricing**, as we have seen, is one method by which suppliers may set their prices: namely, by calculating their costs, then adding on a mark-up or margin to secure some profit. However, we have not yet looked at exactly what costs are included in this calculation. There are two main approaches that suppliers may adopt towards calculating the costs of their products.

- Using a **marginal costing** approach, suppliers concentrate only on the marginal cost of producing additional units for the buyer: basically, they use only variable costs to cost their products. They will therefore have to add on a substantial mark-up, in order to cover fixed costs and earn a profit.
- Using an **absorption costing** approach, suppliers attempt to calculate the total cost of producing products for the buyer, including both variable and fixed costs. They can then simply add a mark-up sufficient to earn a satisfactory profit.

How can a buyer use this kind of supplier cost information?

3.12 The problem with all of this cost analysis is that it is done by the supplier, who may well be reluctant to share the information.

3.13 In the case of a close, long-term supply relationship, there may be a policy of:

- **Open book costing**, where suppliers provide information about their costs to buyers, in order to reassure them that they are getting value for money. In principle, such an approach is helpful in agreeing cost-based prices, and can enable the buyer to help the supplier to identify potential for cost savings. In practice, however, it is unlikely to appeal much to suppliers, because the flow of information is all one way – and to the buyer's advantage.
- **Cost transparency**, where both buyer and supplier share cost information, in order to collaborate in joint cost reduction initiatives. This is arguably a fairer and more mutually advantageous approach than open book costing – but it does demand a high level of trust, which may only exist within long-term partnership relationships.

3.14 In most cases, therefore, buyers will not easily be able to discover details of a supplier's cost structure. However, they may be able to derive some information from a supplier's tender (if a competitive bidding approach has been sued), or may be able to estimate the cost of a supplier's products from their own knowledge of the industry.

3.15 If buyers can ascertain the supplier's cost structure, the information will be useful in negotiating prices. The buyer can assess whether the level of profit targeted by the supplier is excessive: if it is, there is cope for price reduction. Buyers can also:

- Estimate the level of sales the supplier must achieve to break even
- Compare the level of profit targeted by the supplier with that earned by competitors
- Estimate how valuable the business or contract will be to the supplier, in terms of profitability
- Estimate the lowest possible price the supplier can afford to charge.

4   Using competition to obtain quotations

Different approaches to contract award

4.1   A buyer's requirements can be signalled to pre-qualified or approved suppliers in various ways, depending on the type of purchase and company policy.

4.2   The organisation may already have negotiated a **framework agreement** or standing contract with a supplier, to meet a requirement of a certain type. In such a case, the requirement will simply be notified by purchase or call-off order, on the pre-agreed terms.

4.3   There may be only one available supplier, or the organisation may have negotiated a preferred supplier or sole supplier agreement with a dependable supply partner. In such a case, the buyer may simply negotiate a contract with the preferred or designated supplier.

4.4   The organisation may send an 'enquiry' to one or more short-listed suppliers, also called a **request for quotation** (RFQ). The RFQ will set out the details of the requirement: the contact details of the purchaser, the date and requisition reference, the quantity and description of goods or services required, the required place and date of delivery, and the buyer's standard terms and conditions of business. It will then invite the supplier(s) to submit a proposal and price for the job. These may be evaluated:

- On a competitive basis: eg the best value bid or quotation 'wins' the contract (as in competitive bidding or tendering)
- As a basis for negotiation with a preferred supplier. (Note, however, that it is not ethical practice to solicit quotations from more than one supplier if you have already decided where the contract will be awarded – eg just to 'motivate' a preferred supplier.)

4.5   The organisation may have different procedures in place for orders of different volume or value. For order values under $100, say, there may be no formal requirement for supplier selection. For orders between $100 and $5,000, there may be a negotiation process, or three suppliers may be requested to provide quotations, to ensure competitive pricing. For orders over $5,000 in value, a full competitive bidding or tendering process may be required.

Competitive bidding or tendering

4.6   The organisation may prefer to use a *competitive bidding* or tendering procedure, in which pre-qualified suppliers are issued with an invitation to tender (ITT), or an invitation to bid for a contract, with the buyer intending to choose the one submitting the best proposal or the lowest price.

4.7   When should you use competitive bidding rather than a negotiation? Dobler and Burt (*Purchasing & Supply Management*) give the following guidelines for making the decision: Table 2.4.

Table 2.4 *The use of competitive bidding*

FIVE CRITERIA FOR THE USE OF COMPETITIVE BIDDING	FOUR SITUATIONS IN WHICH COMPETITIVE BIDDING SHOULD NOT BE USED
The value of the purchase should be high enough to justify the expense of the process	It is impossible to estimate production costs accurately
The specifications must be clear and the potential suppliers must have a clear idea of the costs involved in fulfilling the contract	Price is not the only or most important criterion in the award of the contract
There must be an adequate number of potential suppliers in the market	Changes to specification are likely as the contract progresses
The potential suppliers must be both technically qualified and keen for the business	Special tooling or set-up costs are major factors
There must be sufficient time for the procedure to be carried out	

4.8 There are several advantages to competitive bidding or tendering. It ensures fairness and genuine competition between suppliers. It ensures that procurement decisions are soundly based on cost and value for money. It also secures a wide choice of suppliers, particularly if open tendering is used.

4.9 However, there are also drawbacks, particularly to open tendering processes.

- Wide competition may discourage potentially suitable bidders.
- There may be inadequate pre-qualification of bidders, creating the risk of capability or capacity problems emerging late in the process.
- Competition based primarily on the lowest price may put insufficient focus on important criteria such as quality and sustainability: the lowest-price bid may not represent the best long-term value.
- Tendering also places a potentially large administrative burden on buyers.
- Contract award may be a one-off, not leading suppliers to expect further business. In other words, tenders do not result in deepening buyer-supplier relationships. This may lead to a widening of the supplier base (whereas the trend is to develop closer relationships with fewer suppliers). There may also be little incentive for suppliers to perform to the highest standard (as a committed, loyal supply chain partner might do), over and above compliance with the minimum standards set by the specification.

The tendering process

4.10 Tendering is the process by which suppliers are invited to put themselves forward (or 'bid') for a contract. There are two basic approaches to this.

- **Selective tendering**, in which potential suppliers are pre-qualified and 3–10 suppliers are short-listed for invitation to tender – as discussed above
- **Open tendering**, in which the invitation to tender is widely advertised and open to any potential bidder.

4.11 A well-established example of open trading is found in the public sector (in the EU). Open competitive tendering is *compulsory* for contracts above a certain value threshold under EU Public Sector Procurement Directives, in order to stimulate fair and open competition.

4.12 Where the buyer has a choice of tendering process, selective tendering will usually be used, because it:

- Is less time-consuming and costly for both buyer and suppliers
- Does not present late problems with technical capability or capacity
- Is less frustrating for non-pre-qualified suppliers who may incur the trouble and expense of tendering without having a realistic change of succeeding.

4.13 A best-practice tender procedure would have the following steps.
- Preparation of detailed specifications and draft contract documents by the procurement department. Once the tender procedure is in motion, there is little room for re-negotiation and adjustment of specifications. Attention must be given to accurate specification of the requirement, so that the buyer's task will be simply to (a) check that tenders received comply with the requirements, and (b) choose the lowest price (or best value) bid.
- Decision on whether to use open or selective/restricted tendering (where not already determined by regulation or company policy)
- Determination of a realistic timetable for the tender process, allowing reasonable time for responses at each stage
- Issue of invitations to tender. In the case of selective tendering, this would be by means of an invitation to bid or request for quotation (RFQ) sent to short-listed suppliers. In the case of open tendering, it would be by means of a public advertisement, with invitations to bid issued to suppliers who respond to the advertisement within the stated time frame. Specifications should be issued to each potential supplier in identical terms and by the same date. It should also be made clear to all tenderers that they are to comply strictly with the timetable for submission.
- Submission of completed tenders or bids by potential suppliers.
- Opening of tenders on the appointed date. Tenders received after this date should be returned un-opened. The tenders received should be logged, with the main details of each listed on an analysis sheet for ease of comparison.
- Analysis of each tender, according to stated criteria, with a view to selecting the best offer. This will usually be on a lowest-price or best value basis, but other criteria (such as environmental compliance or innovation) may be taken into account if clearly notified in the invitation to tender.
- Award of the contract.
- The giving of feedback, on request, to unsuccessful tenderers.

Analysing quotations and tenders

4.14 The general principle is that the successful tender will be the one with the lowest price. However, there is more to it than this. A tender may be on the basis of a performance or functional specification, and there may need to be discussion and analysis to decide whether and how effectively each bid meets the requirements. Even amongst tenderers that do meet the basic requirement, there may be considerable variety in the product and total solution 'package' being offered. One solution may be more attractive (innovative, environmentally friendly, risk-reducing, showing potential for later business development) than another – even if price tells against it.

4.15 It will be important, therefore, for any invitation to tender to state clearly that the buyer will not be bound to accept the lowest price quoted, and that post-tender negotiation may be entered into, if necessary to qualify or clarify tenders, or to discuss potential improvements or adjustments to suppliers' offers.

4.16 The following guidelines summarise the main points to take account of in analysing tenders: Table 2.5.

Table 2.5 *A checklist for analysing tenders*

1	Establish a routine for receiving and opening tenders, distributing copies as appropriate and ensuring security.
2	Set out clearly the responsibilities of the departments involved.
3	Establish objective award criteria. These should have been set out in the initial invitation to tender, particularly if the contract is subject to statutory control.
4	Establish teams for the appraisal of each tender, ensuring that the required team members will be available during the time they are required.
5	Establish a standardised format for logging and reporting on tenders.
6	Check that the tenders received comply with the award criteria. Non-price criteria (eg technical/production capability, financial stability, CSR and environmental policies, or quality assurance accreditation) will need to be carefully reviewed (and more details sought if required), if suppliers have not been pre-qualified.
7	Check the arithmetical accuracy of each tender!
8	Eliminate suppliers whose total quoted price is above the lowest quotes by a specified percentage. (For example, eliminate any supplier whose quoted price is more than 20% above the average of the lowest two quotes.)
9	Evaluate the tenders in accordance with predetermined checklists for technical, contractual and financial details.
10	Prepare a report on each tender for submission to the project manager (and as a basis for feedback to unsuccessful bidders, where relevant).

5 Measuring achieved savings

5.1 The role of procurement can lead not only to significant savings but also to a number of other benefits. Some can be quantified (such as saving money) while others are more intangible (such as improved service delivery). Procurement needs to look at its own efficiency and effectiveness in these areas and put in place performance measures in order to measure achieved savings.

5.2 Savings and benefits typically result from three broad types of procurement.

- **Renewal**: where the term of a contract has ended and it is renewed through a procurement activity. A renewal activity will often have a strong historical baseline that can be used to compare and quantify the savings and benefits the activity creates. Any specification changes should be identified and considered in the comparison. If a product is being offered at a lower specification then the saving is not truly comparable.
- **New buy**: when procuring products or services for the first time, outsourcing existing services or undertaking a one-off procurement activity it can, on the surface, be easy to make savings. 'Our supplier offered us a 20% discount for placing $1 million of business – we have saved $200,000.' New purchase requires an appropriate baseline for comparison such as the budget set in the original business case, otherwise 'savings' when scrutinised can be found to be questionable.
- **Renegotiation or improved terms**: an interaction with an existing supplier that results in savings to the business. This may come from bulk ordering that leads to supplier discounts and rebates, for example.

5.3 Measuring procurement performance is necessary as the procurement department plays an increasingly important role in the supply chain, especially during an economic downturn. A reduction in the cost of materials and services can allow companies to price their own products competitively in order to win business. An obvious performance measure of the success of any procurement department is the amount of money saved by the company. However there are a number of performance measurements that businesses can use when they measure procurement performance.

Procurement efficiency

5.4 Administrative costs are the basis for measuring procurement efficiency. This performance measurement does not relate to the amount of purchased items that the department has procured. The measurement relates to how well the procurement department is performing in the activities they are expected to perform against the budget that is in place for the department. If the procurement costs are within the budget then the efficiency of the procurement department will exceed expectations. If the department is using funds over and above the budget then the procurement function is not efficient.

5.5 Here are some examples of efficiency improvements.
- Staff time saved (including reduced staffing)
- Inventory management
- Implementation of e-tools
- Cultural change
- Demand reduction
- Asset maximisation
- Standardisation
- Employee costs
- Invoicing costs

Procurement effectiveness

5.6 The price that the procurement department paid for an item is not necessarily a good measurement for procurement performance. The price of an item may fluctuate because of market conditions, its availability, and other demand pressures. In other words, the procurement department may not be able to control the price.

5.7 Here are some examples of improvements in effectiveness.
- Capital reduction
- Purchase avoidance
- Price reduction
- Collaborative saving
- Avoiding cost increases
- Added value (eg improved warranties)
- Simplification of specification

Procurement functionality

5.8 Procurement performance can be measured against the functional requirements of the procurement department. The primary function of the department is to provide the correct item at the required time at the lowest possible cost. The performance measurement can take into account these elements, but it does not take into account factors that may relate to supplier stability, material quality issues and supplier discounts.

Performance measurements for procurement

5.9 The performance of the procurement function can be assessed using a variety of measurements. A company can decide which of these measurements of effectiveness are relevant to the performance of their procurement department.

- **Cost savings**
  If the procurement department procure an item at a lower price than they did previously, then it is a cost saving. This can occur when a new supplier is found, a less costly substitute item is used, a new contract has been signed with the supplier, a cheaper transportation method has been found or the procurement department has negotiated a lower price with the existing supplier.
- **Increased quality**
  When an item has improved quality, either through using a different supplier or by negotiating with the existing supplier, the improvement will be reflected in a reduction of waste or production resources.
- **Procurement improvements**
  Efficiencies in the method used in the procurement department will increase effectiveness. These can include for instance the introduction of EDI, e-procurement systems, vendor managed inventory and purchase-to-pay systems.
- **Transportation improvements**
  When a procurement department negotiates with a carrier to reduce the cost of transporting or storing items from the supplier to the production facilities, the unit cost of the item will be reduced. This cost saving can be used as a measurement of effectiveness.

Chapter summary

- Buyers will try to obtain a price that is affordable and gives a competitive advantage.
- Price analysis is the comparison of prices offered by different potential suppliers. Cost analysis is concerned with relating a supplier's price to his costs of production.
- Distributive bargaining means 'dividing up a fixed pie'. Integrative bargaining means 'expanding the pie'.
- Pricing strategies include price volume, penetration pricing, market skimming, contribution pricing, promotional pricing, differential pricing and competition pricing.
- A supplier's costs will typically comprise raw materials, labour and overheads.
- Fixed costs remain unchanged as activity levels increase or decrease. Variable costs rise and fall with changes in activity levels.
- One method of securing good prices is the use of competitive bidding.
- It is important to measure the savings achieved by a procurement function.

Self-test questions

Numbers in brackets refer to paragraphs where you can check your answers.

1. By what means may a buyer obtain a price from a supplier? (1.8)
2. Explain what is meant by cost analysis. (1.14)
3. Distinguish between distributive bargaining and integrative bargaining. (1.21)
4. List some of the external and internal factors that influence a supplier's pricing decisions. (Table 2.2)
5. Explain 'psychological pricing'. (2.6)
6. Distinguish between direct and indirect costs. (3.6)
7. What is meant by open book costing and cost transparency? (3.13)
8. In what circumstances should competitive bidding be avoided? (Table 2.4)
9. List stages in a process for analysing tenders. (Table 2.5)
10. List possible improvements in procurement efficiency. (5.5)

CHAPTER 3
Achieving Quality Supplies

Assessment criteria and indicative content

1.3 Explain techniques to achieve quality supplies
- Defining quality
- Quality standards, processes and procedures
- The use of quality assurance
- The concept of zero defects
- Assessing quality of supplies of products and services

Section headings

1. The right quality
2. Costs of quality
3. Managing supplier quality
4. Quality control
5. Quality assurance
6. Total quality management

Introduction

In this chapter, we start by defining quality, and making the important distinction between quality as 'conformance to specification' (the supplier provides what the customer has asked for) and quality as 'fitness for purpose' (the supplier provides what the customer actually needs).

In Section 2, we go on to look at the costs of quality. Although we are going to focus on each of the five rights in turn, it is important to remember that there are connections and trade-offs between them. The higher the quality of items or services you want, the higher their price will be. Should an organisation pay whatever is necessary for materials and processes to guarantee the best possible quality – or is quality improvement subject to the law of 'diminishing returns', so that there comes a point where it is simply not worth the organisation's while to improve any further?

In Sections 3–6, we examine a range of approaches to quality management, including the crucial distinction (a favourite of examiners) between 'quality control' (detecting and weeding out defective items) and 'quality assurance' (ensuring that you don't have any defective items in the first place), and also the concept of 'zero defects': the belief that it is, indeed, worthwhile for an organisation to aim for no defects at all.

1 The right quality

Defining quality

1.1 Quality is, to an extent, 'in the eye of the beholder'. People have different perceptions about what standard of functionality, durability or presentation is 'acceptable' or makes one product 'superior' to another. Some people may associate quality with a premium price, or a brand label. Others will look more closely at whether the product is well designed or made; whether it functions as it should; whether it lasts well; and so on.

1.2 David A Garvin ('Competing in eight dimensions of quality') identifies eight generic dimensions of product quality.

- *Performance*: the operating characteristics of the product
- *Features*: value-adding characteristics and service elements (such as warranties and after-sales service)
- *Reliability*: the ability of the product to perform consistently over time
- *Durability*: the length of time a product will last (and stand up to normal usage) without deterioration or damage
- *Conformance*: whether agreed specifications and standards are met
- *Serviceability*: the ease and availability of service support
- *Aesthetics*: how appealing or pleasing the product is to the senses of the user
- *Perceived quality*: the subjective expectations and perceptions of buyers.

1.3 However, the 'products' of different organisations vary widely – as do the requirements of different types of buyer. 'Quality' will mean something different for a consumer buying clothes than it will for an industrial buyer of clothing material – or industrial safety wear, say. 'Quality' will mean something different for the purchase of computer equipment, engineering components, building materials, cleaning supplies, accountancy services or catering services.

1.4 Definitions of quality have therefore focused on a range of different dimensions.

- *Excellence*: the degree or standard of excellence of a product; the design, workmanship and attention to detail put into it; and the extent to which finished products are free from defects. (Garvin called this the 'transcendent' approach to quality.)
- *Comparative excellence*: how favourably a product is measured against competitive benchmarks (other products), best practice or standards of excellence
- *Quality of design*: the range of potential customer satisfactions built into a product
- *Fitness for purpose or use*: that is, the extent to which a product does what it is designed and expected to do; or, more generally, the extent to which it meets the customer's needs. (Garvin called this the 'user-based' approach to quality.)
- *Conformance to requirement or specification*: that is, the product matches the features, attributes, performance and standards set out in the specification. Conformance therefore also implies lack of defects, and therefore reflects on the quality of the producer's processes. (The 'product-based' or 'manufacturing-based' approach to quality.)
- *Acceptable quality and value for money*: buyers may be willing to sacrifice some performance and features in order to pay a lower price for a product, as long as it is still fit for purpose. (A 'value-based' approach to quality.)

1.5 For a buyer looking to buy materials, components or other supplies in a commercial setting, the most important definitions of 'right quality' are likely to be fitness for purpose and conformance to specification. Note that both of these criteria are essentially focused on the supplier's ability to satisfy the needs and expectations of the customer or buyer. Van Weele argues that: 'Quality is the degree in which customer requirements are met. We speak of a quality product or quality service when supplier and customer agree on requirements and those requirements are met.'

Fitness for purpose

1.6 The BSI definition of quality is: 'the totality of features and characteristics of a product or service that bear on its ability to satisfy a given need.'

1.7 Fitness for use or purpose was the focus of quality guru Joseph Juran, whose work you may come across in your later CIPS studies. It is also one of the key legal definitions of quality. An example arises in Section 14 of the UK's Sale of Goods Act 1979, which states that where a seller supplies goods in the course of a business, he is bound to provide goods:

- Of *satisfactory quality*: working and in good condition (so far as may be reasonably expected) and free from 'minor defects' (unless these are drawn to the buyer's attention or are obvious to any reasonable pre-purchase inspection)
- *Fit for the purpose* for which they are commonly used, or for any specific purpose made known by the buyer to the seller.

1.8 So an industrial grinder of the 'right quality' is one that grinds. And if the buyer requested a grinder that would tackle a particular material, and grind it to a specific degree of fineness – that is what it should do. In the same way a bucket of the 'right quality' should hold water – and if the buyer asks for a 5-litre bucket, it should hold up to 5 litres of water.

Specifications and quality

1.9 A specification is simply a statement of the requirements to be satisfied in the supply of a product or service. The role of a specification is to define and communicate the buyer's requirements, in terms of either:

- *Conformance*: the buyer details exactly what the required product, part or material must consist of, and a 'quality' product is one which conforms to the description provided by the buyer – or
- *Performance*: the buyer describes what he expects the part or material to be able to achieve, in terms of the functions it will perform and the level of performance it should reach. A 'quality' product is then one which will satisfy these requirements: the buyer specifies the 'ends' (purpose) and the supplier has relative flexibility about the 'means' of achieving them.

1.10 The specification can then provide a means of evaluating the quality or conformance of the goods or services supplied, for acceptance (if conforming to specification) or rejection (if non-conforming).

1.11 The first step for buyers in securing the 'right quality' will therefore be clear and accurate specification of exactly what is required. Essential though this is, however, conformance to specification is not sufficient to secure 'the right quality'. Indeed, it is possible to envisage a situation in which a product conforms to the buyer's specification (is of 'specified quality') – but doesn't do what it is supposed to do, or doesn't perform efficiently, or is difficult to maintain and operate – and is therefore, arguably, not of 'right quality' overall.

1.12 This is a particular risk if the specification is of the conformance type, because supply quality is measured by the extent to which the supplier has complied with the buyer's description or 'prescription' of the requirement: that is, conformance. If the specification itself is limited, vague, inaccurate, incompatible with other elements of the buyer's processes – or just wrong – the work may conform to specification, but still not be fit for purpose.

1.13 The situation is slightly better with performance specifications, because in this case supply quality is measured by the extent to which the supplied goods are able to do what the buyer asks or expects them to do: that is, fitness for purpose. However, they may still be incompatible with the buyer's true requirements in other ways: difficult or costly to use, say, or incompatible with the buyer's other systems – or perhaps quickly rendered outdated and obsolete by technological change. Again, such goods would arguably not be of the 'right quality' from the buyer's point of view.

1.14 An old examination paper gave the example of an organisation buying an expensive scanning machine. Neither the users nor the procurement team were consulted when the specification was drawn up, and it did not take the users' needs and concerns into account. So although the purchased scanner conformed to specification, it was not what the end-users required and was difficult to use. In short, it offered 'conformance', but not fitness for purpose. The organisation incurred added costs of upgrading the scanner, obtaining training for staff and so on.

Services quality

1.15 Most of what we've said so far about 'product quality' also applies to services – and for most of the rest of the chapter, you should think of 'products' as meaning 'products and/or services'. However, in certain important respects, services are not like products.

1.16 Why are services different when it comes to quality definition and management?

- Because services are intangible, it is much more difficult to specify service requirements accurately, and to measure them, when delivered, against specifications and expectations. You can tell if a widget has the right dimensions, shape and colour. But how do you decide what the 'right' architectural design or security service should look like?
- Because services are produced by different people in unique circumstances each time, it is much more difficult to standardise the quality or consistency of service provision. You can make a machine churn out widgets of standard quality. But how do you make one person in one place and time behave exactly the same as another person in another place and time?
- The exact purpose or use of physical goods will usually be known, and their fitness for purpose can therefore be assessed objectively. It is harder to assess the many factors involved in providing a service: what weight should be placed on the friendliness or smart appearance of the supplier's staff, say, compared with the efficiency with which they get the job done?

1.17 Seeking a solution for these difficulties, researchers Parasuraman, Ziethaml & Berry developed an approach to the measurement of service quality which they called **SERVQUAL**. The SERVQUAL model suggests that there are five generic dimensions on which customers evaluate service.

- *Tangibles*: physical products, facilities and results related to the service (eg the smartness of service providers' uniforms and the maintenance of their equipment; the professionalism of documentation provided with the service; the observable state of the office after the cleaners have left)
- *Reliability*: the ability to perform the service accurately, dependably and consistently

- *Responsiveness*: the willingness to help the customer and provide a good level of service
- *Assurance*: the extent to which trust and confidence is inspired in the customer (eg by the competence and conduct of service staff, and the credibility, capability and security of the organisation's systems and procedures)
- *Empathy*: the ability to understand customers' needs, to be approachable, and to offer individual care and attention.

1.18 The important thing to note is that these dimensions lie *in the perception of the customer*. The quality of a given service is the outcome of an evaluation process by which buyers compare what they expected to receive with what they perceive that they have actually received. The SERVQUAL model suggests that there are five distinct areas which might help buyers and suppliers to understand apparent *quality gaps* between expectation and delivery: Table 3.1.

Table 3.1 *SERVQUAL model of 'service gaps'*

GAP	EXPLANATION	BUYER REMEDY
Gap between buyer and supplier perceptions of quality	The supplier's definition of quality may not be the same as the buyer's: he may not know what features represent 'right quality' for the buyer, what features a service must have or what levels of performance are required.	Buyer and supplier will need to work together on developing mutual understanding of the requirement, using service specifications and service level agreements.
Gap between concept and specification	Resource constraints or poor specification skills may mean that either the buyer's needs or the supplier's concept or ideals for a service are not translated fully or accurately into buyer-side or supplier-side specifications.	Buyers will need to co-operate with users and suppliers to develop service specifications which accurately reflect their needs and expectations and the supplier's best capabilities.
Gap between specification and performance	Supplier-side specifications and service level agreements do not translate into actual service levels. Service staff may be unwilling or unable to perform to the specified standard, or work may be poorly organised, supervised or resourced.	The buyer will have to pre-evaluate the supplier's capability to deliver: checking wages paid to staff, supervision and quality management; getting references from other customers; using 'pilot' programmes prior to contract etc.
Gap between communication and performance	The supplier's communications may create inaccurate quality expectations: setting buyers and users up for disappointment (if quality is overstated) or causing them to pass over a suitable supplier (if understated).	Buyers will need to verify information provided by service providers.
Gap between buyer expectations and perceived service	What buyers or users perceive they have received may fall short of what they expected.	Buyers will need to manage user expectations and perceptions; and specify and measure service performance against objective criteria, as far as possible.

1.19 This model clearly illustrates what we said earlier about quality being 'in the eye of the beholder'. This places the specification process at the heart of quality management.

2 Costs of quality

Why is 'the right quality' important?

2.1 It should be fairly obvious that most organisations will seek to maintain the quality of their offerings to their customers, in order to:

- Differentiate their products advantageously in relation to their competitors. The ability to offer consistently high quality may be an important source of competitive advantage for the organisation: quality comparison is likely to be a key decision factor in customer choice between competing products.
- Position their brands in the market as 'quality' brands, potentially allowing them to charge premium prices. Quality is an important factor in corporate reputation and branding.
- Develop customer retention and loyalty: satisfied customers are profitable, because they spend more and more – while costing less and less to reach and serve. Poor quality may lose customers, and also result in negative 'word of mouth' about the product or company.
- Comply with law and regulation (eg in regard to the safety and satisfactory quality of goods)
- Avoid the costs of product recalls, returns and customer compensation, as a result of poor quality
- Maintain the culture and morale of the organisation, and employee satisfaction and loyalty. A culture built on values such as customer satisfaction and excellence is more compelling, positive and pleasant to work in than a culture of indifference, cynicism, 'corner cutting' and constant customer complaints...

2.2 By extension, it is important for an organisation to manage the quality of its specifications and suppliers – and therefore of its materials, components and supplies – in order to maintain the quality of its offering to customers. The quality of the inputs to an organisation's goods and services will naturally affect the quality of its outputs. The ultimate rationale for *buying* 'the right quality' is to be able to *produce* 'the right quality' for customers.

Costs of quality

2.3 The cost of quality has been defined as: 'The cost of ensuring and assuring quality, as well as the loss incurred when quality is not achieved'.

2.4 In other words, quality-related costs include *both*:

- The cost of appraisal and prevention activities, designed to try and minimise poor quality products entering the production process and/or reaching the customer – *and*
- The cost of 'failure': losses incurred because of poor quality products entering the production process and/or reaching the customer.

2.5 Let's look at each of these categories in a little more detail.

Costs of getting quality right

2.6 **Appraisal costs** are the costs incurred as part of the inspection process, in order to ensure that incoming materials – and outgoing finished products – are of the 'right quality'. Here are some examples.

- The cost of physical or machine inspection: the staff required and the investment in machinery for measuring, weighing, sorting and so on.

- The cost of checking incoming materials: setting up and managing inspection processes; checking or testing supplies against specification; and supplier performance appraisal (or vendor rating)
- The cost of quality audits, to check that the quality system is performing as intended.

2.7 **Prevention costs** are those incurred in order to reduce appraisal costs, by preventing or reducing defects or failures produced by the process. Here are some examples.

- The time and cost of building quality into the product or service design
- The establishment of specifications (including cross-functional consultation to define fitness for purpose)
- Developing 'quality circles' (quality problem-solving groups) and other mechanisms for involving staff (and suppliers) in quality issues and improvements
- Setting up processes, systems, technology and training for quality assurance (defect prevention)
- Costs of preparing for auditing and accreditation under international quality management standards such as ISO 9000.

2.8 These costs are obviously substantial. Wouldn't it be more cost effective to spend less on such measures, and simply deal with a few defects now and then? Or won't there come a time when the benefits of improving 'that little bit more' will be outweighed by the costs of doing so? The answer generally given these days is: no. The costs of getting quality wrong may well be higher than the costs of getting it right – and the law of diminishing returns may not apply, because there will always be some benefit to improvement.

Costs of getting quality wrong

2.9 The costs of not achieving the 'right quality' (of incoming materials and/or of finished products offered to customers) can be divided into two categories.

2.10 **Internal failure costs** are those that arise from quality failure, where the problem is identified and corrected before the finished product or service reaches the customer. Here are some examples.

- Loss or reworking of faulty items discovered during the production or inspection process
- Scrapping of defective products that cannot be repaired, used or sold
- Re-inspection of products that have been reworked or corrected
- 'Downgrading' of products (to lower quality grades) at lower prices, resulting in lost sales income
- Waste incurred in holding contingency stocks (to allow for scrapped work and delays), providing additional storage and duplicating work
- Time and cost of activities required to establish the causes of the failure (failure analysis)

2.11 **External failure costs** are those that arise from quality failure identified and corrected after the finished product or service reaches the customer. Here are some examples.

- Costs of 'reverse logistics' to collect and/or handle returned products
- Costs of repairing or replacing defective products (which may be returned by the customer, or require servicing at the customer's location), or re-doing of inadequate services
- The cost of customer claims for compensation under guarantees or warranties, or where the company is liable for negligence (if the customer has been injured or subjected to loss due to defective goods or services)
- The administration costs of handling complaints, processing refunds and so on

- The cost of lost customer loyalty and future sales
- Reputational damage arising from word-of-mouth by dissatisfied customers, poor product reviews and/or publicity (eg about product recalls).

2.12 In addition, we might include costs of **specification failure**.

- Over-specification costs: paying more for materials or components which are better quality or more complex than they need to be in order to be fit for purpose
- Under-specification costs: specifying materials or components which are not good enough for the purpose for which they are required (eg in order to 'cut corners' on price)
- Ineffective specification costs: specifying the wrong materials or components (resulting in fitness for purpose problems) or failing to specify clearly and accurately enough (resulting in conformance problems); and costs of correction, clarification and so on.

2.13 Since the costs of 'getting it wrong' are generally perceived as being higher (and further-reaching) than the costs of 'getting it right', there has generally been an increased emphasis on quality management, with the aim of 'getting it right first time'.

2.14 Be flexible and thoughtful in applying categories of costs in your assessment: remember to respond to the details of the scenario given. In the previous example of the organisation buying the scanner, candidates were asked to give examples of costs incurred by not buying the 'right' (fit for purpose) scanner. Rather then explaining the different classifications (not all of which were relevant), you might have identified specific 'failure' costs such as the need to train staff to use the scanner (not included in the purchase contract); the need to upgrade or replace the scanner to fit it for the user's needs; lost value through staff reluctance to use the scanner; etc.

2.15 Nevertheless, we can summarise the various costs of quality as follows: Figure 3.1.

Figure 3.1 *Costs of quality*

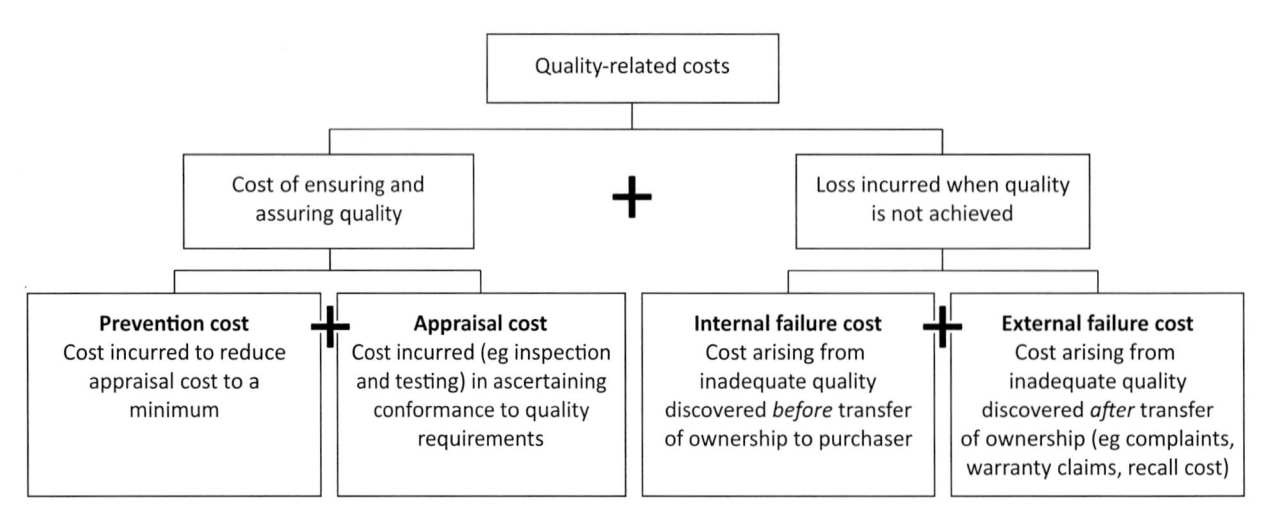

```
                        Quality-related costs
                       /                    \
        Cost of ensuring and    +    Loss incurred when quality
          assuring quality              is not achieved
         /            \                  /              \
 Prevention cost   Appraisal cost   Internal failure   External failure
                                         cost              cost
 Cost incurred    Cost incurred      Cost arising      Cost arising
 to reduce        (eg inspection     from inadequate   from inadequate
 appraisal cost   and testing) in    quality           quality
 to a minimum     ascertaining       discovered        discovered after
                  conformance to     before transfer   transfer of
                  quality            of ownership      ownership (eg
                  requirements       to purchaser      complaints,
                                                       warranty claims,
                                                       recall cost)
```

3 Managing supplier quality

3.1 Although you may come across a wide variety of techniques for managing supply and supplier quality, they generally fall into two basic categories or approaches.

- Systems for the detection and correction of defects: known as **quality control**. This is an essentially reactive approach, focusing on inspection of delivered goods and production

processes. In other words, from the buyer's point of view, you are seeking to identify where a supplier has sent defective products or materials, and to remove them before they get into the production process.
- Systems for the prevention of defects: known as **quality assurance**. This is a more proactive approach, building quality into every stage of the process from concept and specification onwards. From the buyer's point of view, you are seeking to ensure that your buying processes, and your suppliers' quality management processes, work together to prevent defective products or materials ever being delivered.

3.2 The term **quality management** is given to the various processes used to ensure that the right quality inputs and outputs are secured: that products and services are fit for purpose and conform to specification; and that continuous quality improvements are obtained over time. Quality management thus includes both quality control and quality assurance.

3.3 The term **total quality management** is used to refer to a more radical approach to quality management, as a total business philosophy. This is a proactive and all-embracing approach, involving whole organisations and supply chains in the pursuit of continuous improvement and excellence. From the buyer's point of view, the provision of 'the right' quality supplies is only one part of a total quality picture, which also embraces excellent supply chains; continuous collaborative improvement; cross-functional co-operation on quality; and so on.

3.4 We will look at each of these approaches in turn, but first, let's consider in general, practical terms how a procurement function can contribute to providing 'the right quality' to its internal customers (that is, users of supplies and services within the organisation) and therefore also to external customers (on the basis of finished products with quality ingredients, materials or components).

Procurement's contribution to quality

3.5 While the role of the procurement function in many organisations has shifted from 'buying materials' to 'managing suppliers', both of these activities have a significant influence on quality. Dobler et al (*Purchasing and Materials Management*) argue that: 'A designer alone cannot impart quality to a product, nor can an inspector inspect quality into a product. Clearly, quality must be built into a product. It is the buyer's responsibility to ensure that suppliers possess the ability, the motivation, and adequate information to produce materials and components of the specified quality, in a cost-effective manner. In fulfilling this responsibility, a buyer can exert positive control over the quality and attendant costs of incoming material.'

3.6 Quality guru **W Edwards Deming**, in his analysis of Japanese companies, similarly found that such companies were able to maintain high production standards primarily because of their ability to control the *quality of input materials* through close supplier relations, characterised by co-operative quality assurance, the training of supplier personnel and the incentive of long-term relationships. He also argued that considerations such as quality and reliability should be at least as important as price when choosing suppliers.

3.7 Purchasers can thus help to provide 'the right quality' by a wide range of means.
- Selecting suppliers with third party approved or accredited **quality management systems** (eg ISO 9000).
- Appraising and approving suppliers' quality management systems (**supplier certification**):

reviewing design and/or quality assurance documentation; obtaining references from suppliers' other customers; conducting site visits to observe quality systems; sampling output and testing for quality; and so on.
- Making it clear to all suppliers that preference in the award of future contracts will be given to suppliers able to offer reliable quality performance.
- Preparing preferred or **approved supplier lists**, to ensure that user departments only buy from suppliers with appraised quality management.
- Influencing the quality of **product design**, by working with design and production departments (and participating in quality circles, where used); keeping up to date with material developments; recommending alternative materials where appropriate; and facilitating **early supplier involvement (ESI)**, to gain the materials expertise of suppliers in design decisions.
- Translating design requirements into clear, accurate materials and service specifications, reflecting users' needs (fitness for purpose) and specifying required quality standards, measures, inspections and tests.
- Monitoring quality, if necessary, during production: via prototyping, site visits or sampling.
- Developing goods inwards procedures for quality inspection and testing (where necessary in addition to supplier's quality assurance).
- Managing relationships with suppliers: developing a realistic mutual understanding of quality standards and procedures; providing incentives and rewards for high quality and continuous improvement; and so on.
- Monitoring and controlling suppliers' quality performance over time (eg using **vendor rating**); providing suppliers with feedback; and developing closer relationships with reliable quality performers.
- Working with suppliers to resolve quality disputes, solve quality problems and/or make ongoing quality improvements: eg by providing consultancy, training, access to technology and so on (**supplier development**).

3.8 The concept of approved supplier lists and supplier certification arises from the recognition that the quality management systems of a supplier and buyer are really part of the same process. If the buying organisation can be assured that the supplier has already done all the quality control required to supply 'the right quality' inputs, it won't have to duplicate the effort by monitoring or re-inspecting everything on delivery. It can merely check, from time to time, that the supplier's quality management systems are working as they should, by sampling outputs or inspecting procedures and documentation. Integration may be as simple as getting a 'quality guarantee' from suppliers – or there may be detailed formal systems for responsibility sharing, in areas such as specification, inspection, process control, training, reporting and adjustment.

3.9 Let's have a look at some of these quality control and quality assurance techniques in more detail.

4 Quality control

4.1 Quality control is based on the concept of **defect detection**: checking and reviewing work that has already been done, to establish that it offers 'the right quality'.

4.2 This is the most traditional approach to the management of quality, embracing a range of techniques for the following activities.
- Establishing specifications, standards and tolerances (parameters within which items can vary and still be considered acceptable) for work inputs and outputs

- Monitoring or inspecting items at each stage of the supply and production process. This might include: pre-despatch inspection by suppliers; inspection by the goods inwards department on delivery (receiving inspection); inspection during manufacturing or assembly processes (process inspection); and inspection on completion of finished items (final inspection or testing)
- Identifying items that are defective or do not meet specification
- Scrapping or reworking items that do not pass inspection
- Passing acceptable items on to the next stage of the process

4.3 **Inspection** is a key technique of quality control. It involves examining, measuring, testing or otherwise evaluating an item, to check that it conforms to specification and quality requirements in key areas or attributes.

4.4 Many purchasing organisations have a *receiving inspection* department to check incoming deliveries against purchase orders (to ensure correct and complete delivery) and to make a general check of the condition of the delivery (to ensure that there has been no damage during shipment, say), prior to certifying the goods for use.

4.5 There may also be procedures for *technical inspection*, with criteria and methods for inspection – ideally built into the specification, contract or purchase order, so that suppliers know exactly what level of compliance is required. Features of materials may be classified as 'critical', 'major' or 'minor'.

- *100% inspection* may be used on critical features, or where zero defects are required.
- *Sampling inspection* (on items chosen at random from the batch: 1 in every 20 or 1 in every 100 items, say, according to importance) may be used where the costs of 100% inspection are unnecessary or prohibitive.

4.6 You may already be able to see that a quality control approach, based on inspection, has certain limitations.

- A very large number of items must be inspected to prevent defective items from reaching production processes or end customers. Deming argued that this ties up resources – and does not add value (or indeed 'improve' quality).
- Defective items may slip through without being spotted or even inspected, in unacceptable numbers, owing to budget and schedule pressures (especially if the buyer is operating a strategy of just in time supply).
- The process aims to identify and reject defective items once they have already been made. By this time, however, they may already have incurred significant – wasted – costs (of design, raw materials, processing, overheads and so on).
- Inspection activity tends to be duplicated at each stage of the supply process – magnifying the inefficiencies and wastes.

5 Quality assurance

5.1 Quality assurance is a more integrated approach, based on defect prevention. It includes the full range of systematic activities used within a quality management system to 'assure' or give the organisation adequate confidence that items and processes will fulfil its quality requirements. In other words, quality assurance is a matter of 'building in quality' – not 'getting rid of defects'.

5.2 **Defect prevention** systems (such as **statistical process control** or SPC) were proposed by Deming to identify the potential of a process for producing defective items, before such items had in fact been produced. Operating processes are monitored and unacceptable variations in output are identified as soon as they occur. The process is immediately shut down and corrective action taken, preventing the production of further defective items.

5.3 Quality assurance programmes and certification may build quality measures and controls into:

- Product designs
- The drawing up of materials specifications and contracts
- The evaluation, selection, approval and certification of suppliers
- Communication with suppliers, feedback mechanisms and quality record-keeping
- Supplier training and development (where required to integrate the two organisations' quality standards and systems)
- Education, training, motivation and management of employees and suppliers to maintain required levels of performance
- All this would normally be in addition to inspection, sampling, testing and other quality-control techniques.

The concept of zero defects

5.4 In his classic work, *Quality is Free*, **Philip Crosby** argues that: 'A prudent company makes certain that its products and services are delivered to the customer by a management system that does not condone re-work, repair, waste or non-conformance of any sort. These are expensive problems. They must not only be detected and resolved at the earliest moment: they must be prevented from occurring at all.' In other words, no level of defects is acceptable – and any system which potentially allows defects to occur is lacking.

5.5 R Bellis-Jones & M Hand add that: 'Every mistake, every delay and misunderstanding, directly costs a company money through wasted time and effort, including the time taken in pacifying customers. While this cost is important, the impact of poor customer service in terms of lost potential for future sales has also to be taken into account'. The principle that the cost of preventing mistakes is less than the cost of correcting them once they occur – and reach the customer – gave rise to the slogan: 'get it right first time'.

5.6 The concept of zero defects (like 'zero inventory' and 'zero waste') is perhaps more of a cultural value, philosophy or 'ideal aim' than a practical approach: something for an organisation and its supply chain to aspire to and strive for, in order to avoid complacency or indifference, and maintain a 'zero tolerance' towards poor quality. However, there are a number of practical techniques which can help organisations work towards the ideal of zero defects.

- Working with suppliers to integrate quality into every stage of the design, specification and supply process: emphasising 'zero tolerance' for preventable defects
- Developing **quality management systems** (QMS) designed to define and manage processes for systematic quality assurance: discussed further below
- **Failure mode and effect analysis** (FMEA): a technique for determining the different ways (modes) in which a product can fail, and assessing: (a) the probability of failure; (b) the seriousness of the consequences of failure; and (c) the difficulty of detecting failure before the product reaches the customer. This enables the organisation to draw up a 'criticality' index of failure modes, so that it can prioritise resources on eliminating the most critical risks: eg by 100% inspection or testing of critical processes.

- **Ishikawa diagrams** (also known as 'cause and effect analysis' diagrams or 'fishbone diagrams') enabling quality problems to be analysed and identified. The diagrams are basically mind-maps of factors contributing to problems, classified into categories. In manufacturing contexts, these are 5Ms: Machinery, Methods, Materials, Manpower and Maintenance. In non-manufacturing and service contexts, they are 4Ps: Policies, Procedures, People and Plant.
- **Statistical process control** (SPC) by suppliers and the manufacturer: monitoring of processes for early detection of variations, and immediate adjustment before levels of variation are reached that might cause defects. More generally, buyers should be concerned to evaluate the 'process capability' of suppliers: that is, their ability to produce zero-defect work, time and time again.

Benefits of a zero defects approach

5.7 It should be obvious that the main benefit of a zero defect approach is: no defects! But let's recap, briefly, what that means for the organisation in terms of reduced failure costs.

- Fewer product returns and recalls
- Less re-work and scrapped work
- Less likelihood of the production system having to be shut down and readjusted, because of unsatisfactory variances or error levels
- Less potential for damage to the product line from defective items or assemblies
- Reduced likelihood of lost sales, refunds, compensation claims or liability for negligence due to poor quality or unsafe finished goods reaching consumers
- Less reputational damage from product recalls, negative reviews and word-of-mouth and so on
- Reduced total quality costs from these savings – despite the increased costs of appraisal and prevention.

Quality management systems (QMS)

5.8 A quality management system (QMS) can be defined as: 'A set of co-ordinated activities to direct and control an organisation in order to continually improve the effectiveness and efficiency of its performance'. The main purpose of a QMS is to define and manage processes for systematic quality assurance.

5.9 A QMS is designed to ensure that:

- An organisation's customers can have confidence in its ability reliably to deliver products and services which meet their needs and expectations
- The organisation's quality objectives are consistently and efficiently achieved, through improved process control and reduced wastage
- Staff competence, training and morale are enhanced, through clear expectations and process requirements
- Quality gains, once achieved, are maintained over time: learning and good practices do not 'slip' for lack of documentation, adoption and consistency.

Quality standards

5.10 There are several British and international standards for measuring and certifying quality management systems of various types.

- The European Foundation for Quality Management's (EFQM) *Excellence Model* ® is a 'total quality' model, used as a world-class benchmark for quality management. Organisations can carry out self assessments against the EFQM criteria, or apply for quality awards based on them (such as the EFQM Quality Award, or a Business Excellence Award).
- *ISO 9000* is a group of quality management standards laid down by the International Organisation for Standardisation (ISO): a worldwide federation of national standards bodies. ISO 9000 standards deal with quality management systems, with ISO 9001 setting out the requirements, and ISO 9004 offering guidelines for performance improvement. Organisations can use the framework to plan or evaluate their own QMS, or can seek third party assessment and accreditation.

6 Total quality management

Principles and values of TQM

6.1 Following the one-time competitive success of Japanese management techniques, quality management came to represent not just a set of techniques, but a managerial philosophy or ideology – affecting all areas of an organisation's structures and processes. Total quality management (TQM) is an orientation to quality in which quality values and aspirations are applied to the management of all resources and relationships within the firm – and throughout the supply chain – in order to seek continuous improvement and excellence in all aspects of performance.

6.2 Laurie Mullins (*Management and Organisational Behaviour*) synthesises various definitions of TQM as expressing: 'a way of life for an organisation as a whole, committed to total customer satisfaction through a continuous process of improvement, and the contribution and involvement of people'.

6.3 Some of the key principles and values of a TQM approach can be summarised as follows.

- *Get it right first time*. Quality should be designed into products, services and processes, with the aim of achieving zero defects. Taking into account all the costs of poor quality, no proportion of defects can be considered 'optimal' or tolerable.
- *Quality chains*. The quality chain extends from suppliers through to consumers, via the 'internal supply chain' (supplier and customer units representing the flow of work within the organisation). The work of each link in this chain impacts on the next one, and will eventually affect the quality provided to the consumer.
- *Quality culture*. Quality is a 'way of life': a key cultural value in the organisation, which must be expressed and modelled by senior management, and supported and reinforced by recruitment, training, appraisal and reward systems.
- *Total involvement*. Every person within an organisation potentially has an impact on quality, and it is the responsibility of everyone to get quality right.
- *Quality through people*. Commitment, communication, awareness and problem-solving are more important in securing quality than mere systems.
- *Team-based management*. Teams must be empowered and equipped to take action necessary to correct problems, propose and implement improvements, and respond flexibly and fast to customer needs. This requires high-quality, multi-directional communication.
- *Process alignment*. Business processes should be deliberately designed and modified so that every activity is geared to the same end: meeting the customer's wants and needs. Where this is not the case, there may be the need for radical change programmes such as business process re-engineering (BPR).

- *Quality management systems.* Attention is focused on getting processes right. Quality systems should be thoroughly documented in company quality manuals, departmental procedures manuals and detailed work instructions and specifications.
- *Continuous improvement.* Quality improvement is not seen as a 'one-off' exercise. By seeking to improve continuously, organisations stay open to new opportunities and approaches, and encourage learning and flexibility at all levels. In contrast to radical, 'discontinuous' or 'blank slate' change approaches such as BPR, continuous improvement may operate by small-step or incremental changes.

Continuous improvement (*kaizen*)

6.4 Quality management involves the ongoing and continual examination and improvement of existing processes: 'getting it more right, next time'. This process is sometimes referred to by its Japanese name of *kaizen*: 'a Japanese concept of a total quality approach based on continual evolutionary change with considerable responsibility given to employees within certain fixed boundaries' (Mullins).

6.5 *Kaizen* looks for uninterrupted, ongoing incremental change: there is always room for improvement, for example by eliminating wastes (non value-adding activities) or making small adjustments to equipment, materials or team behaviour.

6.6 A basic cyclical approach to *kaizen* may be depicted as follows: Figure 3.2.

Figure 3.2 *Kaizen: continuous cycle of improvement*

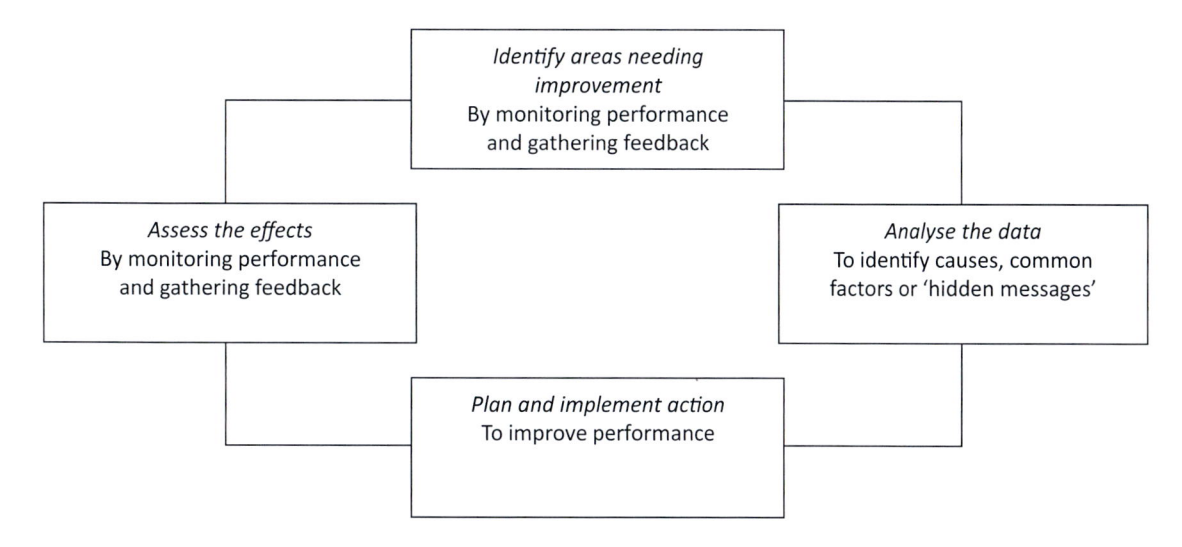

```
           Identify areas needing
                improvement
           By monitoring performance
            and gathering feedback

Assess the effects                    Analyse the data
By monitoring performance             To identify causes, common
 and gathering feedback               factors or 'hidden messages'

           Plan and implement action
              To improve performance
```

Quality circles

6.7 Japanese quality guru **Kaoru Ishikawa** stressed the importance of people and participation in the process of solving quality problems. He devised the idea of *quality circles*: a voluntary-participation team of employees from different levels and functions in an organisation, which meets regularly to discuss issues relating to quality, share best practice and recommend improvements.

6.8 In practice, quality circles may or may not have significant responsibility for making, implementing or monitoring the progress of their recommendations. Even as discussion groups, however, they can have significant benefits: harnessing the expertise of different functions and levels of the organisation; overcoming resistance to quality management and creating quality 'champions'; improving communication and information-sharing on quality issues; and general support for a quality culture.

6.9 You should be able to see the advantage of purchasing staff being able to discuss issues of quality management with designers, engineers and users: gaining an insight into users' needs; proposing materials and supplier management solutions; and so on. The quality circle concept has been expanded to include:

- Quality groups drawn from a wider range of participants and stakeholders in the supply process – including suppliers and customers.
- Best-practice sharing groups or networks, which may include a wide range of organisations with a common interest in quality issues.

Why doesn't everybody practise TQM?

6.10 Total quality management may sound like such a good thing that you wonder why every firm isn't implementing it! Here are a few suggestions as to why this is the case.

- TQM can prove limited in practice. The initiative may be poorly introduced or managed, and therefore ineffective. Short-term benefits of introducing TQM may wear off over time, as people get complacent or bored.
- TQM can be disruptive, if it is introduced as a transformative change – leaving people unsure about what to do, or what to do next. The extent and trauma of the change required should not be underestimated.
- TQM is time-consuming, costly and difficult to introduce, implement and 'settle in' – particularly in large, bureaucratic organisations which may resist new cultural values such as customer focus and employee involvement.

6.11 You will encounter TQM and related concepts in more detail later in your CIPS studies. For this exam, the syllabus focuses on concepts most closely related to the buyer's point of view: the need to secure 'the right quality' of materials.

Chapter summary

- Quality can be assessed in many different ways. As an example, Garvin identifies eight dimensions of quality.
- Most commentators are agreed that quality lies in the perception of the customer. However proud we may be of the technical excellence (say) of our products, if they do not provide customers with exactly what they want, they cannot be said to have quality.
- There are significant costs involved in achieving quality (eg appraisal costs and prevention costs). There are also costs involved in failing to achieve it (internal and external failure costs).
- Quality control involves systems for the detection and correction of defects. Quality assurance is better: it involves systems for the prevention of defects.
- There are many contributions that procurement can make to achieving quality, such as selecting suppliers with suitable accreditation.
- Quality control involves inspection of output, either on a sampling basis or for all items.
- Quality assurance involves techniques such as statistical process control. Its aim is to achieve zero defects.
- Total quality management is an orientation to quality in which quality values and aspirations are applied to the management of all resources and relationships within the firm.

Self-test questions

Numbers in brackets refer to paragraphs where you can check your answers.

1. What eight dimensions of quality are identified by Garvin? (1.2)

2. Why are services different from products when it comes to quality definition and management? (1.15, 1.16)

3. List examples of appraisal costs, prevention costs, internal failure costs and external failure costs. (2.6, 2.7, 2.10, 2.11)

4. Distinguish between quality control and quality assurance. (3.1)

5. List ways in which procurement can contribute to achieving quality. (3.7)

6. List techniques of quality control. (4.2)

7. By what means can an organisation work towards zero defects? (5.6)

8. Give some examples of quality management systems. (5.10)

9. List the key principles of TQM. (6.3)

10. What are the stages in a cyclical approach to continuous improvement? (Figure 3.2)

CHAPTER 4

The Right Quantity at the Right Time

Assessment criteria and indicative content

1.4 Assess techniques to secure required quantities at required timescales
- Internal, external and total lead time
- Expediting and measuring delivery performance
- Planning milestones and activities
- The use of scheduling
- Inventories and their costs

Section headings

1. Inventories and their costs
2. Forecasting demand
3. Scheduling
4. Lead times
5. Managing supplier delivery performance

Introduction

In this chapter we look at 'the right quantity' and 'the right time'.

You might wonder why these two topics are covered together, while the other 'rights' are covered separately. As we will see, quantity and time are inextricably linked in a buyer's decision-making.

Issues such as 'demand' and 'stock levels' are as much a feature of time decisions as they are of quantity decisions. If you are purchasing supplies to cover demand over a long time period, you will need a larger quantity. If you purchase in small quantities, you will need to re-order more frequently. If you think you might need stocks of an item at short notice (because customer demand might peak unexpectedly), you might buy a large quantity well in advance, so that you have extra stock available if needed. Alternatively, you might wait and only top up with a small quantity when you need to – but then the turnaround time for the order will need to be short.

If you buy in large quantities, there is a time dimension: it will take longer to use up the stock – and this means higher costs of storage, and more risk of damage or deterioration. If you buy in small quantities, there is a time dimension: you are more likely to run out of stock in the face of unexpected demand, and then the 'right time' will be 'as soon as possible'.

1 Inventories and their costs

Factors in the decision of how much to buy

1.1 What is the 'right quantity' to buy in a given situation? Of course, it varies. If you receive a requisition from the operations manager to replace one worn lathe, say, the 'right quantity' is one. If a bill of materials for a customer order specifies 2,000 subassemblies, the 'right quantity' is 2,000 subassemblies. But what if your company produces cars: how many components will it need in a given period? How much oil will it need to lubricate its assembly line? And what if you receive that requisition for one lathe – but you know that another lathe will become worn out shortly: is it more advantageous to buy one lathe now, or two? Buyers will have to work with users and inventory managers to establish the optimum quantity (and timing) of purchases for a given situation.

1.2 Lysons & Farrington suggest that the most important factors determining the 'right quantity' to purchase in a given situation are as follows.

- *Demand for the final product* into which the purchased materials and components are incorporated (dependent demand). Obviously, the more cars you anticipate selling, the more wheels you are going to have to buy – and if you are planning to produce 1,000 cars in a given period, you will need 4,000 wheels in the same period.
- *Demand for purchased finished items*, such as office equipment and supplies, computer hardware and software or maintenance services (independent demand). This may be based on past and average usage and replacement rates, for example. If your office gets through an average of 60 reams of paper per month, you will probably plan to purchase a similar quantity on a monthly basis.
- *The inventory policy of the organisation*: whether its main aim is to secure service levels by holding safety stocks (as a 'buffer' against unforeseen demand or supply difficulties) – or to minimise or eliminate stocks, to avoid the costs and risks associated with holding stock
- *The service level required*: whether an item must be available in full on demand 100% of the time (eg for critical production items or hospital supplies) or only 90–95% of the time (eg for routine supplies)
- *Market conditions*, affecting the price and security of supply, which dictate whether requirements must be 'stockpiled' to secure supply or take advantage of low prices, or can be bought on an *ad hoc* or opportunistic basis
- *Supply-side factors*, such as minimum order quantities or values, or price incentives for bulk purchases
- *Factors determining the economic order quantity (EOQ)* which balances the costs of acquiring stock (higher with frequent smaller orders) against the costs of holding stock (higher with fewer larger orders)
- *Specific quantities notified to buyers by user departments, according to identified needs*. For example, the operations function may indicate required quantities for a particular job or application via materials specifications or a bill of materials (BOM). Standard items, consumables and spares may be ordered by purchase requisitions from user departments or stock control staff. Computerised inventory reports (or the electronic point of sale systems in a retail organisation) may specify re-order quantities when inventory gets down to a predetermined level, in order to 'top up' stock in line with anticipated demand.

1.3 We will look at a range of these factors, as we proceed through this chapter. Most of them are within the control of the buying organisation: forecasting demand, analysing stock requirements and costs and so on.

Minimum order quantities (MOQ) and values

1.4 For some suppliers, it is simply not worth supplying very small quantities to buyers, particularly if the items have a very low unit price; the norm is to sell in bulk; and items are packaged accordingly. (Examples might include small industrial items such as nuts and bolts, small stationery products, cleaning supplies, lubricants and so on.) The breaking of bulk, counting out of small quantities, and the administrative processing of the order and payment would mean that the transaction cost to the supplier would offset – and perhaps even exceed – the value of the order.

1.5 The supplier's policy in such a case would be to set a minimum order quantity and/or a minimum order value, which ensures that the value of the order is greater than the transaction cost of fulfilling it – and that the supplier therefore makes some profit on the deal.

1.6 A buyer faced with a minimum order quantity or value in excess of his requirements will have to decide:
- Whether the minimum quantity will be usable over time (and before it is likely to perish, become obsolete or deteriorate in storage): if not, the purchase will result in waste.
- Whether there is adequate storage capacity for the minimum quantity, at reasonable cost, while it awaits usage: if not, the purchase will be simply impracticable and/or unacceptably costly in relation to its value.

1.7 If the minimum order quantity is a problem, for either of these reasons, the buyer may have to 'get around it': by finding an alternative supplier or a substitute product (where available); or by negotiating with the supplier for special terms. It may, for example, be possible to pay for the minimum order quantity (or to pay the minimum order value), but to obtain the items on a 'call off' basis: in other words, the supplier reserves the goods and sends them in small consignments, when orders are called off against the original purchase contract.

Inventory management

1.8 Inventory management covers a variety of activities.
- *Demand management*: ensuring that supplies are available in the right quantities at the right time for the needs of internal (and external) customers
- *Forecasting demand* (and therefore supply requirements) in order to avoid over-stocking
- *Controlling stock levels* (in terms of quantity and value held), and monitoring and maintaining target minimum and maximum stock levels – to avoid over-stocking and production 'bottlenecks' due to stockouts
- Ensuring that supplies are *replenished* in accordance with procurement policies
- Developing cost-effective *systems and procedures* for ordering and procurement of supplies
- *Controlling* the receipt, inspection, storage and issuing of supplies to users and
- Ensuring that stocks are *safe and secure* from deterioration, damage, theft or obsolescence.

Prioritising stock decisions: ABC analysis

1.9 Vilfredo Pareto (1848–1923), an Italian economist and sociologist, formulated what has been called the **Pareto principle** or '80:20 rule': 'in any series of elements to be controlled, a selected small factor [20%] in terms of number of elements almost always accounts for a large factor [80%] in terms of effort'. Applied to supply data, the Pareto principle means, roughly speaking, that 80% of the total 'usage value' of stock will be accounted for by 20% of the stock items. Usage value is calculated as the unit cost of an item multiplied by its annual usage rate.

1.10 Refining this principle further, ABC analysis divides stock items into three categories.

- *Category A* items: the 'vital few'. Small in number, but high in usage value – and therefore the focus of most managerial control effort.
- *Category B* items: 'normal items'. Medium in number and usage value.
- *Category C* items: the 'trivial many'. High in number, but low in usage value – and therefore the focus of the least managerial control effort.

1.11 This offers a simple way of prioritising stock items according to their relative value. More attention will be given to monitoring and managing inventory levels of Category A items than Category B or C items, because this is where over-stocking and under-stocking make the most impact. Management attention can thus be focused on the areas where it really matters.

Reasons for holding stock

1.12 There are a number of reasons why an organisation would want to hold stock or inventory.

- Stocks reduce the risk of disruption to production from unforeseen events. 'Safety' or 'buffer' stocks allow the organisation to keep working if supply is disrupted by strikes, transport breakdowns, supply shortages, supplier failure and so on. Stock 'buys time' for purchasers to find alternative sources of needed materials. This is particularly important for items which are critical for operations: it would be disastrous if a firm ran out of such items, and some stock must be held in order to avoid this.
- Stocks reduce the risk of disruption to production from long or uncertain delivery lead times. Suppliers' production and delivery lead times cannot always be known accurately in advance, so stock in hand allows the organisation to keep working (and maintaining service to its customers) if replenishment takes longer than anticipated.
- Stocks allow rapid replenishment of goods which are in constant use and demand, such as maintenance and office supplies.
- Buyers may be able to take advantage of bulk discounts, lower prices or reduced transaction costs by placing fewer, larger orders, for quantities in excess of what is immediately required.
- Buyers may be able to protect against anticipated shortages, price increases, or exchange rate fluctuations, by buying (or 'stockpiling') goods at advantageous terms, or while available, in advance of requirement.
- Stocks of finished or almost-finished goods may be prepared ready for unexpected peaks in customer demand – or for the **late customisation** of products to customer specification. (A popular example is that of Dell computers, which builds up stock of finished computer models, which can simply be assembled swiftly and flexibly according to customers' requirements.)
- Stocks of finished goods may be prepared during periods of slow demand, ready to meet peaks of demand which are beyond the organisation's production capacity: in effect, 'smoothing out' peaks and troughs in production.

1.13 In particular, the organisation will want to avoid stockouts: that is, being out of inventory of a required item. Stockouts are costly because of: lost production output and idle time (due to the unavailability of materials or components); overhead costs still being incurred, with reduced production to cover them; loss of credibility, trust and customer goodwill through delayed delivery of finished items; non-delivery or late delivery penalties; and the costs of dealing with the stockout (such as high-priced 'emergency' purchases).

Reasons for minimising stock

1.14 So far, we have looked at reasons for holding stocks – but there are also good reasons for *not* holding stocks, or at least for *minimising* the level (quantity and value) of stocks. One of the most important reasons is that stockholding incurs costs.

- There are costs in *acquiring* stock: the cost of setting up and maintaining an information system for procurement; and the cost of procurement procedures each time an order is placed (preparing purchase requisitions, selecting suppliers, preparing purchase orders and other documentation, receiving and inspecting incoming deliveries; processing payment; and so on).
- There are costs in *holding* stock: the capital tied up in the stock (ie the purchase price); the 'opportunity cost' of having capital tied up in stock when it could be used to earn interest; the costs of storing inventory (rent and rates on warehouse space, insuring the stock, materials handling machinery, and the wages of warehouse or stores staff); and the cost of losses through damage, deterioration, pilferage and obsolescence while goods are being held.

1.15 **Acquisition costs** actually decrease as stock levels rise, because it is cheaper to make fewer, larger orders. But **holding costs** increase as stock levels rise. There is a genuine trade-off here. This has given rise to the concept of *economic order quantity (EOQ)*, which balances acquisition and holding costs to identify the quantity of a given item which should be regularly ordered in order to minimise its total cost to the firm. The general point, however, is that there is a fine line between the costs of holding stock – and the costs and risks of not having sufficient stocks to meet the firm's needs, and customers' requirements.

Buffer (safety) stocks

1.16 Buffer stock (or 'safety stock') is a reserve of stock sufficient to take care of situations where demand or usage is above the foreseen or average rate, or when supplier delivery periods exceed normal or anticipated lead times. In other words, safety stock is a 'cushion' or 'buffer' to protect the organisation from potentially damaging effects of uncertainties in both demand (more needed than usual) and supply (longer lead times).

1.17 What level of safety stock will be sufficient to cover the organisation's needs? The main factors in the selection of safety stock levels include the following.

- *Required service levels*. If a particular department requires a particular component and a stockout would have serious effects, a service level of 100% might be prescribed (requirements met immediately, in full, on demand, every time). In less critical cases, the required service level might be set at, say, 90%: the department is supplied with 900 out of 1,000 components on demand, or is provided with the full 1,000 components on demand, 9 times out of 10. The higher the service level, the more inventory must be held to be certain of meeting it.
- *Variability of demand*. If demand is uncertain and/or fluctuating, there is a greater probability of stockout: sufficient safety stocks may be required to maintain service levels in the face of the highest anticipated level of demand.
- *Variability of supply*. If supply, or supplier lead time for delivery, is uncertain and/or

fluctuating, there is again a greater probability of stockout: sufficient safety stocks may be required to maintain production during the longest foreseeable lead time to obtain stock.
- *Probability, costs and consequences of stockouts*. For critical items, which would cause bottlenecks in production if unavailable, it will be particularly important to hold safety stocks. For non-essential items, which can be readily obtained (and/or temporarily done without), it will be less important to hold safety stocks.
- *Costs of holding stock*. Safety stocks may be generous for items which are of low value, and do not require much space or special handling. They are likely to be less generous, all other things being equal, if they are expensive to hold.
- *Company policy*. Most such decisions will have already been made, and there should be policies and parameters in place for the levels of safety stocks of each item or category of item, to which buyers can simply refer.

2 Forecasting demand

Dependent and independent demand

2.1 The ability to forecast demand accurately is crucial for ascertaining what the 'right' quantity of stock will be at a given time.

2.2 Many stock items are subject to *dependent demand*: that is, the extent to which the item is used depends on the exact volume and nature of the production schedule for a larger item of which it forms a part. Dependent demand items are therefore typically subassemblies or components used during the production of the finished product. Demand is dependent on the specification and number of finished units being produced: it can thus be accurately measured on the basis of production schedules and materials requirements. For example, if 1,000 units are due to be manufactured, and each unit requires five sub-modules, then we will need to order 5,000 sub-modules.

2.3 Other stock items will be subject to *independent demand*: not linked to production of another finished item. The amount of oil required to keep a machine in working order does not depend on which products are being processed on that machine: it should simply be possible to identify that a certain (average) amount of oil is used each day, week or month. The same may be true of purchases such as office equipment and supplies, computer hardware and software, motor vehicles, marketing services, maintenance services and so on.

2.4 The distinction between dependent and independent demand is important because some inventory control systems are designed to meet dependent demand (forecasting the materials requirements for a specified type and level of production), while others are more suited to general *stock replenishment*, in response to independent demand.

Forecasting techniques

2.5 Forecasting is an essential part of all planning and decision-making, and accurate forecasting of demand, in particular, is vital for ensuring that the right quantities of supplies are available at the right time.

2.6 Various statistical techniques can be used to forecast demand. You shouldn't have to use them in the exam, but you should be aware of what they involve.

- **Simple moving average**: assuming that demand for a coming period will be 'average', that is an average of the demand recorded in recent past periods. So if usage of a given material from January to June ran at 450, 190, 600, 600, 420 and 380 units, we might anticipate that July's usage would be an average of these six months: 2,640/6 = 440 units. The reason this is called a moving average is that each month we move along by one step: in forecasting August's demand, for example, we would take an average of usage in February to July. This isn't a very accurate method, as it doesn't take into account the fluctuations hidden by the average: in our example, actual demand could be anywhere from 190 to 600 units.
- **Weighted average** (or **exponential smoothing**): giving extra weight to more recent data in calculating the average, and less to earlier data: adding some accuracy by reflecting more recent trends.
- **Time series (trend) analysis**: examining past demand data in chronological order, identifying underlying trends (long-term upward or downward movements over time) and projecting these trends into the future. It may also be possible to identify repeated seasonal variations (eg peak demand periods at certain times of year) and cyclical variations (eg peaks and troughs of demand in an industry), which can be taken into account in forecasting. However, there may also be random fluctuations, due to one off events or environmental factors: no statistical analysis can account accurately for every variation in demand patterns.
- **Regression analysis**: identifying connections between measured variables (such as advertising spend or price increases and sales levels) and predicting the effect of changes in one variable (eg increasing advertising or lowering prices) on the other (hopefully, increased sales).

2.7 Statistical methods are unlikely to be able to take into account all the various environmental factors which may cause fluctuations in demand. A number of more subjective or 'qualitative' methods may therefore be used, based on personal information gathering and judgement by managers.

- **Marketing and/or customer research** can be used to ascertain potential interest and demand, particularly in new products, or to help identify trends in sales and the reasons behind them.
- **Expert opinion** is the gathering of views, judgments and opinions from people regarded as knowledgeable and experienced in relevant business areas.
- **The Delphi method** (named after an ancient Greek oracle) gathers expert opinion using postal or email questionnaires, removing the risk – common in expert opinion panels – of people being influenced too early by each other's ideas.

3 Scheduling

'Push' and 'pull' inventory strategies

3.1 Inventory control systems generally fall into two categories: 'push' systems and 'pull' systems.

- Push systems aim to provide supplies of materials in anticipation of demand: production is often based on long-term forecasts, for which demand is uncertain. Push-based systems are characterised by stock management methods such as periodic review and fixed order quantity (discussed below), where demand is forecast in advance and stock levels are kept to predetermined levels in order to ensure that anticipated levels of demand can be met. They often involve relatively high inventory levels, owing to the need to respond to demand changes.
- Pull systems are based on producing goods in response to actual demand (in the form of

customer orders). Buyers place orders with suppliers as and when items are required for production. In such a system, demand is much more certain: inventory can therefore be relatively low – or even non-existent. Perhaps the most well known 'pull' approach is just in time (JIT) supply.

3.2 The aim of 'push'-style inventory management, for independent demand items, is to set up a regular system for monitoring levels of stock, and planning to replenish them in time to meet forecast demand (the right quantity at the right time). In other words, we attempt to schedule the orders to be placed with suppliers.

3.3 There are two main methods for doing this and we will look at each in turn.

- Periodic review systems, in which the stock level of an item is reviewed at regular or fixed intervals, and, depending on the quantity in stock, a replenishment order is placed for whatever quantity appears to be appropriate.
- Fixed order quantity systems, in which stock of an item is replenished with a predetermined quantity when inventory falls to a predetermined re-order level (ROL) or fixed order point

Periodic review

3.4 In periodic review systems (also called *fixed interval ordering*, *scheduling* systems or *'topping up'* systems), the stock level of the product is examined on a periodic (fixed time interval) basis, and, depending on the quantity in stock, a replenishment order is placed to 'top up' stock to the desired level. In other words, the order quantity is not fixed, but the timing of orders is. Replenishment quantities vary, being whatever is sufficient to bring stock levels up to a predetermined stock level – or whatever is needed to last through the next interval, or until the next delivery. This can be depicted simply as follows: Figure 4.1.

Figure 4.1 *Periodic review system*

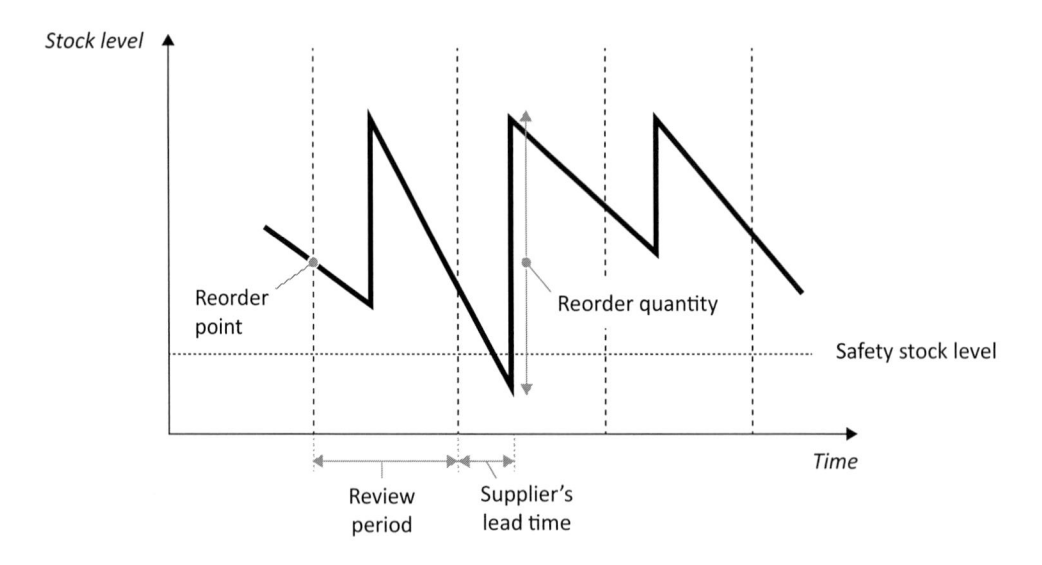

3.5 The length of the review period will be determined on an item-by-item (or category-by-category) basis, depending on usage patterns. The shorter the review period, the more effort and cost is involved, so it is usual to apply an ABC analysis: Category A items might be reviewed weekly, Category B items monthly and Category C items quarterly, say.

3.6 The review itself can be undertaken by periodic physical inspection by stores staff ('stocktake'), or by a computerised or manual system that records ongoing purchases, requisitions and returns of each item to give a running total of stock held at any given time. (This latter system is sometimes called **perpetual inventory**, because it is carried out on a constant basis.) Computerised systems often use *barcode* scanning to input stock data to the system. A more modern alternative is **radio frequency identification** (RFID): an electronic tagging system which does not require item-by-item scanning to input stock data, but simply 'reads' the signals given out by electronic tags on stock.

3.7 Once the current stock level has been established at a given review point, the decision must be taken on how much to order to replenish the stock to a desired level. Take a monthly review system, for example. At the 1st January review point, an order will be made based on the quantities of the item likely to be required during January; *plus* enough stock to cover the lead time for delivery following a review and order on the 1st February; *plus* an appropriate level of safety stock.

3.8 In other words, the size of the order will be calculated as: forecast demand over the forthcoming review interval; *plus* forecast demand over the lead time for replenishment (ordering and delivery) in the following review interval; plus safety or buffer stock; minus current stock levels; *minus* stock already on order but not yet delivered.

3.9 Lysons & Farrington express this mathematically as:

$M = W(T + L) + S$

where 'M' is the predetermined stock level; 'W' is the average rate of stock usage; 'T' is the review period; 'L' is the lead time; and 'S' is safety stock.

In the example they give, the average rate of usage is 120 items per day; the review period is 20 days; the lead time is 25–30 days; and safety stock is 900 items.

$M = 120(20 + 30) + 900 = 6,900$ items.

If at the previous review period, current stock was 4,000 items, an order would be placed for 2,900 items, to 'top up' to the predetermined maximum stock level of 6,900 items.

3.10 The *advantages* and *disadvantages* of a periodic review or fixed interval ordering system can be shown as follows: Table 4.1.

Table 4.1 *Advantages and disadvantages of periodic review*

ADVANTAGES OF PERIODIC REVIEW	DISADVANTAGES OF PERIODIC REVIEW
Ease of administration and control, with predictable workload planning for procurement and warehousing staff (at fixed review/replenishment periods)	The risk of unexpected stockouts, since the system assumes that there will be no review of stock other than at the fixed interval. This necessitates the use of safety stocks.
Orders may be placed at the same time for a number of items, enabling the consolidation of shipments, reduced transport costs, or quantity discounts from suppliers	Higher average stocks than with fixed order point systems, because of the need to provide for review periods, lead times and safety stocks
Ability to identify slow-moving or obsolete stock items, due to periodic stock review.	Re-order quantities not based on economic order quantities (EOQs)
	Waste of time reviewing stock levels which do not require action.

Fixed order quantity and re-order level (ROL)

3.11 In a fixed order quantity (or re-order point) system, stock of an item is replenished with a predetermined (fixed order) quantity when inventory falls to a predetermined minimum level (the re-order level or ROL). In other words – directly opposite to the periodic review approach – the timing of the order isn't fixed, but the quantity is. The system can be depicted simply as follows: Figure 4.2.

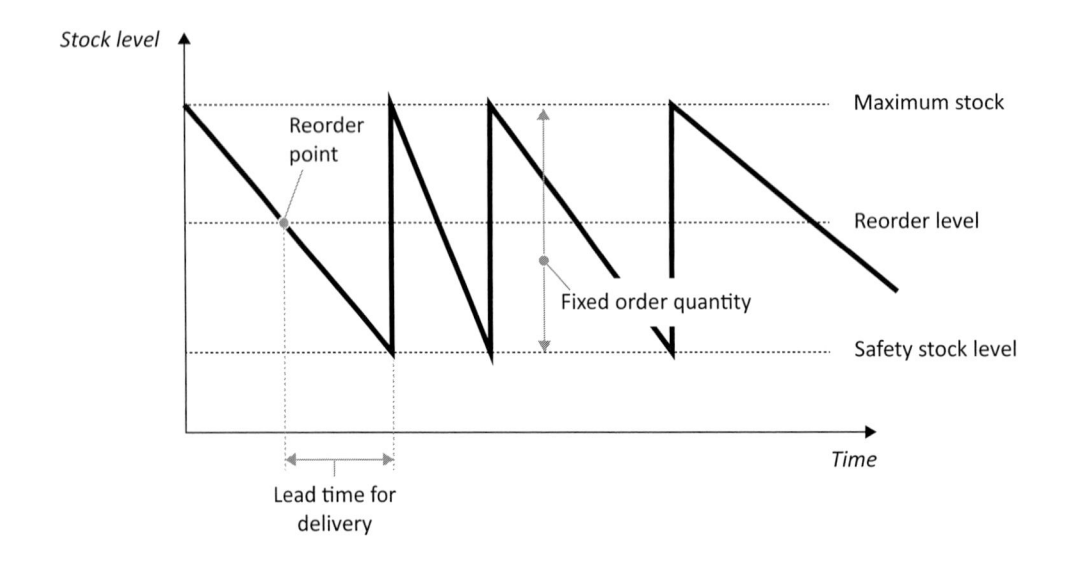

Figure 4.2 *Fixed order quantity systems*

3.12 To determine the re-order point for a particular item, managers rely on past experience of demand or usage patterns for the item, taking into account any known factors which may lessen or increase demand or usage in the coming period. The aim is to fix on a stock level sufficient to keep the business in stock during the supplier's delivery lead time, plus a reserve of safety stock. In other words, a basic re-order level (ROL) should be equal to:

- Maximum amount used × maximum lead time for replenishment
  or
- (Average amount used × average lead time) + safety stock

3.13 Once stock falls to this predetermined order point or ROL, the system triggers a replenishment order.

- A common manual method for doing this is a *two-bin system*. For each stock item, two bins are maintained. The first is immediate stock in use, while the second contains the amount of stock determined as the ROL. When the first bin is empty, you know automatically that you are down to the ROL, and it is time to re-order. While waiting for the order to be delivered, the contents of the second bin are used. Ideally, this bin will be down to safety stock level when the delivery comes in, and both bins are replenished from the order.
- Computerised perpetual inventory systems (using barcoding to record inputs and withdrawals of stock and maintain running totals) may be used to automatically trigger replenishment orders when inventory has fallen to the specified re-order point.

3.14 In either case, the re-order quantity is the same each time. For items of high value, it may be sensible to use a structured approach to determining what this should be, perhaps by using the economic order quantity (EOQ) – described below. For small-value items, simple decision rules (based on usage rates) may be more cost-effective.

3.15 *Advantages* and *disadvantages* of a fixed order quantity or ROL system can be summarised as follows: Table 4.2.

Table 4.2 *Advantages and disadvantages of fixed order quantity or ROL systems*

ADVANTAGES OF FIXED ORDER QUANTITY/ROL	DISADVANTAGES OF FIXED ORDER QUANTITY/ROL
Ability to use the EOQ, unlike periodic review systems	Acceptance of the holding cost (which may be expensive if the stock levels are set too high)
Lower average levels of stock than with periodic review systems, because of enhanced responsiveness to demand fluctuations	Assumption that stock usage patterns and lead times are predictable and stable. Parameters must be reviewed, to avoid risk of stockouts (if demand is higher, or lead time longer, than foreseen) – or excess stock (eg if replenished in full, despite fall-off of demand).
Automatic 'triggering' of replenishment by the system, without time being wasted on items where the stock level is satisfactory.	Inefficiencies, from inappropriate order points and quantities and/or from ordering of individual items at different times. Eg: frequent uneconomical small orders.
	Risk of overloading procurement systems and staff, if multiple items reach their re-order levels at the same time.

Economic order quantity (EOQ)

3.16 As we have already seen, there are significant costs incurred in acquiring and holding stock.
- **Acquisition costs** are incurred when orders are placed: costs of management time, administration, paper work and transaction charges.
- **Holding costs** include the cost of working capital tied up in stock; the costs of storage; and the costs of damage, deterioration, pilferage and obsolescence while goods are being held.

3.17 The task of the procurement manager is, ideally, to reduce these costs – but note that there is an inherent trade-off between them.
- You could seek to minimise *acquisition* costs by making fewer, larger orders – but this would increase your stock levels, and hence your holding costs.
- You could seek to minimise your *holding* costs by only purchasing stock in small quantities, as and when you need them – but this would increase the frequency of your orders, and hence your acquisition costs.

3.18 How is this dilemma resolved? There will be a certain order quantity at which holding costs will equal acquisition costs – and the total cost will be as low as possible: this is called the economic order quantity or EOQ. (There are various ways of calculating EOQ mathematically, but that would take us beyond your syllabus.)

3.19 The EOQ model is helpful in establishing the most economical order quantity for high-value items, as part of a fixed order quantity system. However, it does suffer from certain limitations.
- It is based on assumptions about the consistency of demand, order quantities and supplier lead times – which may not always be valid in practice.

- It is a cumbersome method to apply, and should only be used if justified by the value of the item being examined.
- Some of the costs (such as clerical time, interest rates and order costs) are difficult to estimate.
- The model does not take into account price breaks and bulk discounts – nor other factors in optimum order quantities, such as the perishability of stocks, or the transport efficiencies of larger orders.

4 Lead times

What is the 'right time' for delivery?

4.1 We have already seen that the 'right time' for delivery depends to a large extent on the buying organisation's policies about holding stock.

4.2 On the one hand, it is straightforward to say that goods must be 'on time': that is, not late for a production or delivery deadline. Late delivery deadlines set by a purchaser, or late deliveries by a supplier, may cause the following problems.

- Production 'bottlenecks' and stoppages, as machines or assembly lines wait for required supplies
- Costs associated with idle time (while waiting for delivery) and/or seeking out alternative 'emergency' supplies
- Late delivery of finished goods to the organisation's end customers, with attendant loss of trust, credibility and goodwill (and potentially, therefore, future business), and possibly also late delivery penalties.

4.3 On the other hand, as we saw above, it is not necessarily a good thing for purchasers to set 'early' delivery deadlines (that is, to secure supplies before they are required for use) – because of the costs of holding stock, the risk of obsolescence and deterioration of goods in stock, and the difficulty of accurately forecasting demand in advance. The 'right time' may be 'just in time' for requirement.

4.4 Moreover, there is an increasing emphasis on 'responsiveness' to customer demand – essentially, a 'time' factor – as an important source of competitive advantage. Organisations that can respond swiftly to customer orders, or to changing environmental factors, by getting hold of supplies at short notice, are able to offer customers leading edge products (because of the speed of getting products to market); swift, flexible service (because of the ability to fill customer orders quickly); and perhaps product customisation (because of the ability to finish or assemble orders to customer specification quickly). The 'right time' may therefore be a matter of supply chain responsiveness or agility: speed and flexibility of action.

Understanding supplier lead times

4.5 The expression 'lead time' has a number of different meanings, and it is important for users and purchasers to understand the true or total length of the lead time to obtain goods, when operating demand management or stock replenishment systems.

- The **internal lead time** is the lead time for the processes carried out within the buying organisation: that is, the time between the identification of a need and the issue of a completed purchase order. This might therefore include the preparation of a specification; the identification and selection of suppliers; contract negotiation and so on.

- The **external lead time** is the lead time for the processes carried out within the supplying organisation: that is, the time between the supplier receiving the purchase order and fulfilling that order (by delivering the goods). It might therefore include process development, manufacture, despatch and delivery time.
- The **total lead time** is therefore a combination of internal and external lead time: that is, the time between the identification of a need by the buyer to delivery of goods by the supplier. As the most comprehensive definition, this is the safest lead time to use in planning to obtain goods at the 'right time'.

4.6 Baily et al also note that different parties in a transaction – users, purchasers and suppliers – may have different perceptions about what lead time means, and it will be important for all parties to be 'on the same page' when discussing lead times. They depict the various perceptions as follows: Figure 4.3.

Figure 4.3 *Different perceptions of lead time*

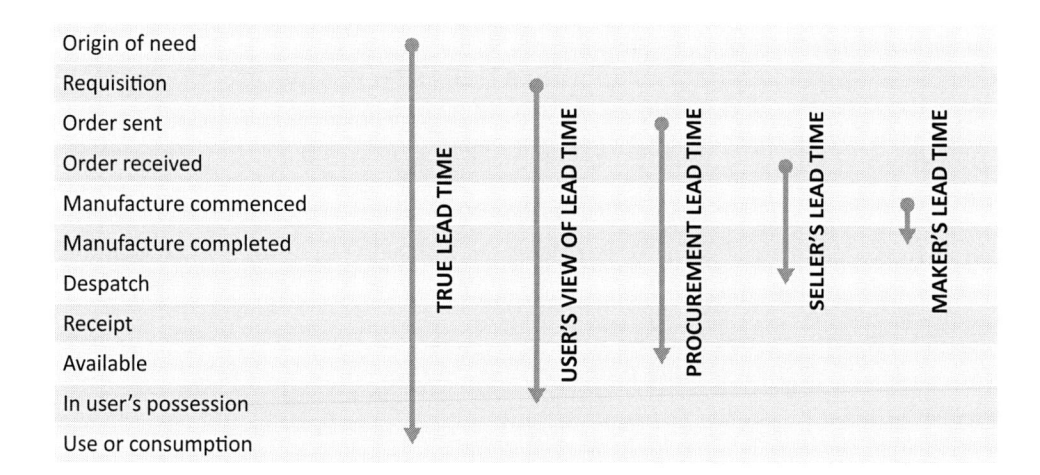

Stage	True Lead Time	User's View of Lead Time	Procurement Lead Time	Seller's Lead Time	Maker's Lead Time
Origin of need	↓				
Requisition		↓			
Order sent					
Order received			↓		
Manufacture commenced				↓	
Manufacture completed					↓
Despatch					
Receipt					
Available					
In user's possession					
Use or consumption					

4.7 So if the supplier's production manager talks about a six week lead time, he may only be referring to manufacturing time. And if the buying organisation's production manager talks about a six week lead time, the purchaser will need to add (to his own view of lead time) time to prepare a requisition or specification – and any time lag between receipt of goods and actually getting them to the production line. Note that there may be a considerable time lag between delivery or receipt of the goods (procurement's usual target); their availability (following goods inwards procedures, quality inspections, breaking of bulk and so on); their reaching the user (after inter-site delivery, perhaps); and their use or consumption (after setting up of production machinery, say, or holding in stores until required).

Are supplier-quoted lead times realistic?

4.8 Baily et al note that: 'Sometimes suppliers quote delivery dates which they cannot achieve. This may be an unscrupulous device to get the order, or the quote may be given in good faith but circumstances change and delivery dates are rescheduled. Sometimes the firms which fail to deliver on time may not be competent at production planning and control. Frequently, of course, purchasers are themselves the source of the delivery problem, through issuing inaccurate delivery schedules, continually amended, or by allowing insufficient time for delivery.' (*Purchasing Principles and Management*).

4.9 How can you check whether a supplier's quoted lead time is realistic? You should be able to ascertain whether the supplier:

- Has sufficient available production capacity (including machine time, labour and materials) during the period in question.
- Has a credible and reliable track record of delivery performance (either with your firm, through keeping delivery records, or with other customers, by obtaining references).
- Has credible production planning systems (especially if these are integrated with the demand management systems of the buying organisation, so that there is accurate advance warning of requirements)
- Has its own supply strategies in place to ensure availability of materials and components for production: sufficient stocks of long lead-time supplies, for example, and a flexible and secure supply base.

Reducing lead times

4.10 We have so far focused on ensuring that realistic total lead times are taken into account. But what if a purchaser wants to reduce or shorten a lead time, in order to obtain an urgent delivery of supplies – or to make the supply chain generally more responsive (eg so that it can operate just in time supply or late customisation)? There may be various options for shortening lead times, at different levels.

- Negotiating incentive prices for 'priority' or 'urgent' orders, for unusually swift turnaround and delivery by suppliers.
- Streamlining transaction and information-sharing processes (eg by integrating computer systems with regular supply partners)
- Working collaboratively with external and internal supply chain partners to reduce 'waste' time at all stages of the supply process: unnecessary waiting and idle time; unnecessary transport, handling or processing operations; and so on. Quality assurance by the supplier, for example, may shorten inspection time at goods inwards.
- Negotiating contracts with supply partners to pre-manufacture and hold stocks of work in progress (eg subassemblies), which can be more swiftly assembled and finished in response to demand: this is a key approach to late customisation, for example.

5 Managing supplier delivery performance

Planning milestones and activities

5.1 Achieving on-time delivery is one of the key objectives by which the performance of the procurement function is measured. How, then, do purchasers go about ensuring that suppliers deliver by the date specified in the purchase order or contract? They should:

- Ensure that user departments (and purchasers themselves) understand the concept of 'lead times', and how long it will take from purchase requisition to delivery – in order to avoid unrealistic expectations and last-minute requisitions
- Check that lead times quoted by suppliers are realistic, given the demands of the job and the capability of the supplier
- Select suppliers with a good capability and track record of delivery performance
- Ensure that suppliers understand the importance of on-time delivery, and what the required service level is (eg 95% or 100% on-time in-full deliveries): this should be a key criterion in the monitoring, recording and measurement of supplier performance (as discussed below)

- Stipulate in purchase contracts that 'time is of the essence': that is, that the delivery deadline is a 'condition' or important term of the contract.
- Issue accurate, precise and realistic delivery schedules to suppliers – and stick with them, avoiding disruptive or confusing changes to schedules or requirements.
- 'Expedite' deliveries: that is, monitor their progress and chase them up if necessary (as discussed below)
- Give regular suppliers advance notice of ongoing requirements, supporting their production planning by providing accurate demand forecasts (perhaps through integrating planning systems with regular long-term supply partners).
- Establish relationships with 'agile' suppliers who are able to respond quickly and flexibly to unexpected, short-notice demand.

Specifying and measuring delivery performance

5.2 Clear expectations should be set out in each purchase order as to precise delivery dates and penalties for late deliveries. In addition, for ongoing supply contracts, the buyer will need to include delivery performance as a key criterion for supplier performance appraisal and management.

5.3 Supplier management and performance measurement is a huge topic in itself. Briefly, however, there are various approaches to monitoring delivery performance.

5.4 For suppliers who make regular deliveries, a simple informal approach is as follows.

- To keep records of supplier success or failure in delivering on time; what proportion of deliveries are on time or late; and by how many days they are late
- To use this information to guide supplier selection decisions: analysing which suppliers have better, worse, improving or worsening delivery performance, and giving preference to suppliers with the best (or improving) track record
- To feed this information back to suppliers, to let them know: that delivery performance is taken seriously; how they are doing; and how their performance needs to be improved.

5.5 Baily *et al* suggest that 94% on-time service levels can be achieved when suppliers:

- Are made to realise that requirement dates, as stated on orders and call-off schedules, are *accurate*: that is, that the buyer takes them seriously
- Are reminded that whenever they fail to deliver on time, they will be required to explain the reason why
- Are made to realise that on-time delivery will be taken into account in the award of future business.

5.6 Defined **key performance indicators** (KPIs) or performance measures for delivery may be included in the supply contract or service level agreement. Here are some typical KPIs for delivery performance.

- The number or percentage of orders delivered on-time in-full (OTIF).
- The number or percentage of orders delivered within the acceptable tolerance range (eg within, say, three days of the contracted delivery date)
- The number, percentage or frequency of late deliveries (perhaps broken down by tolerance bands: less than 3 days late, 3–7 days late, 7–14 days late, more than 14 days late).

5.7 **Vendor rating** is the term given to formal appraisal of the performance of a supplier, across a range of criteria: price, quality, delivery and so on. In a simple checklist system, the supplier's delivery performance (defined as 'delivery on schedule') would be evaluated as 'good', 'satisfactory' or 'unsatisfactory'. In a more complex scoring system, delivery would be given a weighting (according to its perceived importance), and the supplier would be numerically scored on delivery: say, as a percentage of on-time orders. If a supplier only delivered on time 82% of the time, for example:

Performance factor	*Weighting*	*Supplier's score*	*Supplier rating*
Price	0.4	0.94	0.376
Quality	0.4	0.97	0.388
Delivery	0.2	0.82	0.164
Overall evaluation	1.0		0.928

5.8 The supplier in our example has achieved a rating of 0.928 out of a possible 1. This score can be compared with that achieved by other suppliers, and gives a good measure of exactly where each stands in the order of preference. It may also be used year on year, to provide a measure of whether a supplier's performance is improving or declining.

Expediting orders

5.9 'Expediting' simply means 'assisting the progress' of something. If the buyer has any concerns about delivery (because the supplier is less than reliable, or because on-time delivery is critical), the order may require expediting.

5.10 Expediting may be as simple as a buyer's making a phone call to the supplier to check on progress – and it may be natural for the buyer to be responsible for managing timing and delivery, if he has been dealing closely with the supplier on an order. However, a team of full-time expediters may be employed to manage the timing of supply (especially for a complex project, for example): they may be attached to the buying department, or project planning or a user department (which has a strong grasp of schedules and priorities).

5.11 The term 'progress chasing' or 'order chasing' is sometimes used instead of 'expediting': usually meaning an enquiry into how progress is going, or (more often) where an order is when it is late. However, this is a reactive or 'fire fighting' approach, focused on problem solving rather than problem avoidance. Expediting should ideally be a proactive role, as an ongoing part of **contract management**: taking planned steps to ensure that suppliers are able and on schedule to deliver as agreed in the supply contract.

5.12 Not all orders will be worth the effort and cost of expediting, so the first requirement will be to prioritise deliveries, identifying those for which:

- There is a higher risk of delivery problems (because the supplier is unknown to the buyer, or has a poor or variable delivery track record)
- The potential consequences of delivery problems are more severe (because the material is critical to production processes or schedules; or the organisation has low safety stocks; or because there are no alternative sources of supply or substitutes for the item concerned).

5.13 Expediting tasks may then consist of:
- Ensuring that delivery deadlines and specifications are clearly set out – and, if any changes are made, that these are clearly communicated and agreed
- Maintaining project and production schedules, and time-phased materials requirements (eg in a materials requirements planning system). A project expediter may maintain critical path network charts and/or Gantt charts showing the optimum and latest times at which supplies are required for each stage of the project. For regular supplies, a simple diary system may be sufficient to 'flag' which orders need to be expedited on a given day or week
- Monitoring or enquiring about supplier progress at key stages (without 'micro-managing'), or developing a system of 'reporting by exception' (where the supplier notifies the expediter of any stage deadlines missed or potential problems identified)
- Working with suppliers to solve any identified problems. The expediter may have to persuade a supplier to give priority to the order or buying organisation; offer help with production difficulties; offer help in sourcing any materials or information which may be holding the supplier up; and so on.
- Requiring notification of despatch of goods, and using track and trace facilities (where available) to monitor their progress in transit
- Placing pressure on poorly performing suppliers, where required: reminding them of late delivery penalties (eg liquidated damages clauses), say, or involving senior managers in problem-solving or enforcement discussions.
- Where necessary, using contingency plans to search for alternative suppliers, existing stocks or substitute goods to meet an emergency shortage due to delivery delay.

> **Chapter summary**
>
> - Determining the right quantity involves consideration of many factors, including estimated demand, inventory policy, required service levels etc.
> - ABC analysis is used so as to focus management attention on the small number of stock items that are high in usage value.
> - There are many reasons for holding buffer stocks, but such stockholding incurs costs – this must be balanced against the need for production efficiency and customer service.
> - Ensuring the right quantity involves forecasting demand, which may be done by statistical techniques or more subjective methods.
> - Stock replenishment systems include periodic review (check at a predetermined interval of time, and top up to the extent needed), and fixed order quantity (order the same quantity every time, when stock falls to a predetermined level).
> - The economic order quantity is the amount which minimises the total of acquisition costs and holding costs.
> - Total lead time is a combination of internal lead time and external lead time. Both must be taken into account when determining 'the right time'.
> - Buyers must specify and measure a supplier's delivery performance to ensure 'the right time'. Even then, there may be a need for expediting activities.

Self-test questions

Numbers in brackets refer to paragraphs where you can check your answers.

1   List factors to be considered when deciding on order quantities. (1.2)

2   Explain what is meant by Pareto analysis. (1.9–1.11)

3   List factors to be considered when deciding on a level of buffer stock. (1.17)

4   Distinguish between a simple moving average and a weighted average in the context of forecasting demand. (2.6)

5   Distinguish between push and pull systems of inventory control. (3.1)

6   Distinguish between periodic review and fixed order quantity approaches to stock replenishment. (3.3)

7   Explain what is meant by internal lead time, external lead time and total lead time. (4.5)

8   What checks can be made to determine whether a supplier's quoted lead time is realistic? (4.9)

9   What steps can buyers take to secure on-time delivery? (5.1)

10 What tasks are typically involved in expediting? (5.13)

CHAPTER 5

Identifying Procurement Needs

Assessment criteria and indicative content

2.1 Explain how procurement needs are identified

- Liaison with users and customers and understanding their commercial needs
- Reviewing needs from customers
- The make or buy decision
- Definitions of specifications

Section headings

1. Liaison with users and customers
2. Buyer and supplier contributions
3. Information requirements for specification development
4. Influences on specification development
5. The make/do or buy decision

Introduction

In this chapter we look first at the process of specification development, and different approaches by which this can be organised, including the need for cross-functional input. We then look at the different contributions made by buyers and suppliers to the specification process – and what happens if buyers do not 'take control' of the process.

We then look at a range of influences on specification development and decisions: the information required; the different stakeholders in specification and how they influence the process; and the influence of company policy in various areas.

Finally, we look at the make or buy decision.

1 Liaison with users and customers

Defining a specification

1.1 A specification can be simply defined as a statement of the requirements to be satisfied in the supply of a product or service. In the following chapter we will look at this in more detail, and explain the different types of specification that exist. For the moment, though, this simple definition is enough for our purposes.

1.2 As part of the purchase cycle, the role of a specification is to:

- *Define the requirement* – encouraging all relevant stakeholders (including the purchasers and users of the supplied items) to consider what they really need, and whether what they think they need is the only, most cost-effective or most value-adding solution

- *Communicate the requirement* clearly to suppliers, so that they can plan to conform – and perhaps also use their expertise to come up with innovative or lower-cost solutions to the requirement 'problem': in other words, so that you get what you need.
- *Provide a means of evaluating the quality or conformance* of the goods or services supplied, for acceptance (if conforming to specification) or rejection (if non-conforming).

1.3 A specification is often thought of in terms of the 'right product or service' at the 'right quality' – but it may also include other aspects of the 'five rights' requirement, including the quantity required, and when and where delivery is required.

Features of effective specifications

1.4 The process of preparing specifications is unlikely to be uniform in every case. This is true even within a single organisation, and even more so if one organisation is compared with another. We will look at some general principles in this chapter, but it is worth you looking for specific examples from your own work organisation, to gain more understanding.

1.5 An effective specification is one that is:

- Clear and unambiguous as to what is required
- Concise (not overly detailed: the shorter the specification, the less time and cost it takes to prepare) but
- Comprehensive (covering all points of the requirement. As Lysons & Farrington note: 'If something is not specified, it is unlikely to be provided'. Suppliers will normally charge requirements added later as 'extras'.)
- Compliant with all relevant national or international standards, and health, safety and environmental laws and regulations
- Up-to-date (with current design solutions and supply market developments)
- Expressed in terms which can be understood by all key stakeholders (ie not too technical for suppliers or purchasers or users)
- Value-analysed: every additional requirement increases the price, so it is important to specify only requirements that positively add value.

Cross-functional contributions

1.6 In most cases, the lead role in specification development is taken by users of the product (often designers or engineers) or service. After all, they may be most familiar with the requirement, and most technically 'savvy' about what is required. But this is not always the case.

- For many purchases, the process is relatively simple: the quality required is easy to define in terms of products widely available on the market. In such cases, it would be normal to leave the 'specification' (ordering) to the procurement department.
- Another situation where the procurement department would usually have a free hand is in cases of purchases for internal use, rather than resale or incorporation into production. Examples cited by Baily, Farmer, Jessop and Jones (*Purchasing Principles and Management*) include factory seating and overalls.
- Procurement departments may also take a lead role where procurement staff are technically expert in the product or category specified (eg knowledgeable about grades, standards and so on).

1.7 In less straightforward cases, however, the preparation of a specification may require *cross-functional input*, so that technical considerations are balanced with commercial ones.

1.8 Design or *engineering departments* will be well placed to contribute technical specifications. However, they may:

- Focus on features that maximise functional excellence (a product orientation), or production efficiency (a production orientation) – but contribute little or nothing to sales potential or customer satisfaction (a marketing orientation)
- Over-specify, with unnecessarily tight tolerances or non-value-adding functions, in pursuit of quality or engineering excellence – but at unnecessary cost
- Specify bespoke or custom-built items, when acceptable standard or generic items are available. This may arise from lack of knowledge of the supply market, or lack of attention to costs
- Specify for each new requirement, even where existing items could be used or adapted to the purpose – creating multiple stock items where one would do, and thus incurring unnecessary inventory, ordering and materials handling costs
- Write 'narrow' or 'closed' specifications, not permitting variations or alternatives, which may tie the buyer to a small supplier base, or one supplier – or which may be very difficult to source

1.9 The *marketing department* may be able to contribute an important customer focus to the specification: seeking unique product features which will delight customers and gain competitive advantage for the firm. However, marketing suggestions may not meet technical and cost criteria: customer-satisfying and customised features may be difficult to engineer and/or costly.

Reviewing needs from customers

1.10 Reconciling these differences requires skilled management. Dobler and Burt (*Purchasing & Supply Management*) identify four major items that have to be brought into harmony.

- Design considerations of function
- Marketing considerations of consumer acceptance and satisfaction
- Manufacturing considerations of economical production
- Procurement considerations of markets, materials availability, supplier capability and cost.

1.11 It is obviously in this latter area that the purchaser's role is most significant. Procurement departments are in a good position to make the following contributions.

- *Supply market awareness*: the availability of standard or generic items (for variety reduction), the availability of capable suppliers, the possibility of alternative suppliers and solutions (especially if expensive branded products are requisitioned), market prices, supply market risk factors, availability issues
- *Supplier contacts*, to discuss potential solutions in advance of specification, or to introduce pre-qualified suppliers to the design team (early supplier involvement), which may in turn improve technical specification
- Awareness of *commercial aspects* of purchases, eg the need to include requirements for just in time (low inventory) supply or supplier stock holding, response times, maintenance cover, spares availability, warranty periods and user training in the specification
- Awareness of *legal aspects* of purchases, eg the need to comply with national and international standards, and regulations on health and safety, environmental protection and (in the public sector) procurement methods.
- Procurement *disciplines*, for variety reduction, value analysis, cost reduction and so on. The buyer should be ready to discuss the real needs of the user, and to question desired

performance levels or tolerances, to pursue gains in these areas. The greatest scope for cost reduction is at the design and specification stage.

Approaches to specification development

1.12   Dobler and Burt describe four possible approaches to organising the specification process.

- *Early buyer involvement (EBI)*. Management recognises from the outset that procurement contacts and disciplines are important in product development. Procurement specialists are involved in the product development team, on an advisory or full-time basis.
- *Formal committee approach*. Management recognises from the outset that preparing a specification is a matter of reconciling conflicting objectives. They appoint a committee with members representing each key stakeholder: design, engineering, production, marketing, quality management and procurement.
- *Informal approach*. Management emphasise the responsibility of all departments to consider both commercial and engineering factors. Buyers are encouraged to challenge the assumptions of users, and to suggest alternative methods and materials for consideration. Designers are encouraged to seek advice from buyers before going too far down any particular design path.
- *Procurement co-ordinator approach*: a formalisation of the informal approach, with procurement staff designated as 'liaison officers' to co-ordinate the required communication.

1.13   Whatever approach is used in preparing the specification, it is advisable to ensure controlled *signing off* procedures. Before a specification is released to a supplier, it must have the formal approval of the procurement department and ideally the prior certification of the supplier. This reduces the common risk of changes being made in order to solve problems not envisaged at the time the specification was finalised. This precaution should then be followed up by ensuring that any changes which are deemed necessary are subjected to appropriate approval procedures and documented in writing.

2 Buyer and supplier contributions

Who should drive the specification?

2.1   As we have seen, a key purpose of the specification is to describe the buyer's requirements. A specification driven by buyer-side requirements places the buyer clearly in control of the procurement process.

- The supplier is left in no doubt as to what must be done to perform the purchase contract satisfactorily.
- Legally, goods supplied which fail to conform to the buyer's specification can be rejected and not paid for.

2.2   If the *supplier* drives the specification process, by defining what it can offer (eg in the case of specification by brand name or purchase from a product catalogue), or its solution to the requirement 'problem', the buyer takes on additional risks.

- The specification may be highly technical, based on the supplier's expertise, and may not be clearly understood by the buyer, or susceptible to meaningful measurement and evaluation.
- The requirement is defined in terms of what the supplier can offer, rather than what is actually needed (as defined by buyer-side designers, users and other stakeholders): the buyer may not get exactly what he wants or needs.

- The buyer will be unable legally to reject goods which are not suitable or relevant, but comply with specification: if he attempts to do so, he will be liable for a claim of breach of contract.

2.3 A specification should state clearly that it is a description of the buyer's requirements; what the acceptable tolerances are; and that no substitutes, alternatives or variations will be acceptable without the buyer's express agreement.

The buyer's role in specification

2.4 In general terms, the buyer's role in the specification process may include:

- *Understanding the needs of users*: ensuring that user requirements have been consulted (as the primary stakeholders in the purchase) – but also challenged, if necessary, to avoid over-specification and to promote variety reduction and cost reduction.
- *Liaising with users*: working with users on the development of specifications (to add commercial know-how and disciplines); ensuring that users approve the final specification prior to contracting; communicating policies for user-department purchasing (eg using call-off contracts or framework agreements); working with users to monitor and measure compliance of the delivered goods or services with the specification; gathering feedback with users as to whether the specification meets the requirement or may need to be updated.
- *Minimising the tolerances*: supporting quality management by ensuring that tolerances are minimised as far as possible, consistent with value added and cost incurred. For most engineering processes, the aim will now be 'zero defects' or 'get it right first time', which means negotiating and managing tight tolerances with suppliers – as well as within the production process of the buying organisation.
- *Understanding the legal implications of specification*: ensuring that the specification, and the contract upon which it is based, accurately and completely expresses users' requirements (minimising the risk of legal disputes and contract variations); and recommending performance rather than conformance specifications, where possible, in order to transfer legal liability for non-performance to the supplier.

2.5 As we saw earlier, there are significant benefits to involving purchasers at the specification stage – and potential problems if procurement input is not taken into account. The term **early buyer involvement** (EBI) is used to describe a process whereby procurement specialists are involved in defining specifications – rather than merely turning specifications, prepared by users, into purchase orders. Where this is not the case, the procurement function may need to 'promote' its expertise and potential contribution, in order to obtain greater input.

2.6 Where EBI is implemented, procurement specialists may act in an advisory capacity to product development teams, or may be integrated into the project team on a full-time basis, or a procurement co-ordinator may be allocated to the team to liaise with the procurement department. Procurement experts may provide the design and specification team with the following contributions.

- Input to make/do or buy decisions: which technologies should be kept or developed in-house and which should be outsourced
- Policy formulation for supplier involvement and internal procurement
- Monitoring of supply markets for technological developments
- Pre-selection of suppliers for involvement in the development project
- Supplier relationship management
- Ordering and expediting of samples and prototypes from suppliers

- Information on new products and technologies already available or being developed
- Suggestion of alternative suppliers, products or technologies that could yield greater value
- Evaluation of product designs in terms of parts availability, manufacturability, lead time, quality and costs
- Promotion of standardisation, variety reduction and simplification.

The supplier's role in specification: early supplier involvement (ESI)

2.7 The concept of **early supplier involvement** (ESI) is that organisations should involve suppliers at an early stage in the product or service development process: ideally, as early as the conceptual design stage, although this is not always practical. This contrasts with the traditional approach, whereby the supplier merely provides feedback on a completed product design specification.

2.8 The main purpose of ESI is to enable a pre-qualified supplier (with proven supply and technical abilities) to contribute technical expertise which the buying organisation may lack, by making proactive suggestions to improve product or service design, or to reduce the costs of production. There are numerous ways in which suppliers can contribute to the product development process. For example, they can provide constructive criticism of designs, and suggest alternative materials or manufacturing methods at a time when engineering changes are still possible.

2.9 Dobler and Burt cite numerous areas where supplier expertise can benefit the buyer: material specifications; tolerances; standardisation or variety reduction; economic order sizes to reduce costs; packaging and transportation requirements for the product; inventory levels (taking into account lead times); potential changes required in the supplier's manufacturing and/or the buyer's assembly processes to maximise quality or achieve cost savings.

2.10 In service contracting, it is common for the potential service provider to collaboratively develop and negotiate service specifications and service level agreements as part of a cross-functional team with users and purchasers.

2.11 The benefits to be gained from ESI have mainly focused on relatively short-term organisational gains via more accurate and achievable technical specifications, improved product quality, reduction in development time, and reduction in development and product costs. However, there may also be some long-term benefits. ESI can, for example, be a catalyst for long-term, partnership relationships with excellent suppliers. It can also improve the buyer's understanding about technological developments in the supply market, with potential for further exploitation.

2.12 As with most approaches, practitioners also need to be aware of potential drawbacks. The product or service may be designed around the supplier's capabilities, which (a) may be limiting, and (b) may lock the buyer into a supply relationship. This may become a problem if the supplier becomes complacent and ceases to deliver the quality or innovation he once did – or if market developments present better alternatives. In addition, ESI may pose confidentiality and security issues (eg the risk of leakage of product plans to competitors).

3 Information requirements for specification development

3.1 If a purchaser (or cross-functional team) is asked to prepare a specification for a product or service, what information will they need to do this effectively? This is not quite the same question as 'what information will go into the specification?' It concerns the information that will have to be gathered to support the decisions and choices that go into drawing up the specification.

Technical requirements

3.2　The first and most basic information to be gathered is the precise technical requirements of the product or service to be purchased. As we have seen, in our discussion of technical specifications, this may include:

- Intended function or performance: what the product or service must be able to do
- Conditions under which the product or service will be required to operate, be transported, handled and stored
- Measures of quality and performance
- Tolerances for reliability, quality, dimension, strength and other key properties
- Features: texture, colour, aesthetics, finishing and other external properties
- Durability (the useful life of the product) and serviceability (speed, ease and cost of maintenance)
- Information provided with the product or service (eg operating, maintenance and safety instructions).

3.3　This information will come primarily from the designers, engineers and users of a product, or the users of a service, who are likely to be most expert in their own needs. Input may also be sought from other sources.

- Suppliers of goods and services, who may have additional technical expertise
- In-house providers of a service (if the service is being outsourced)
- Third party experts (eg engineering, IT, systems design, security or logistics consultants)
- Industry contacts, such as other firms using similar products or services – and even competitors (eg by 'reverse engineering' or analysing the composition and functionality of their successful products)
- Industry, national and international standards, which set out technical requirements for a range of items used for different purposes.

Availability of commercial products or services

3.4　Potential sources of supply are not directly mentioned in the syllabus content as one of the information requirements for preparing specifications, and you might agree that this is an item that could wait until the specification had been developed. However, it may be useful information at this stage because:

- If there are no (or few, or inaccessible) existing sources of supply, the technical specification may need to be reviewed for feasibility
- If there is a reliable and high-quality source of supply, it may be possible to involve the supplier in the specification, to improve the quality of supply market information (early supplier involvement)
- Users may have specified items to be manufactured specially to their design ('bespoke' or 'made to order' items), while a survey of the potential supply market may identify a readily available commercial or standard item which will do the job just as well. Commercial products and services are more quickly accessed and less costly (because they do not include customisation and development costs, and because there may be more than one supplier, allowing price negotiation).

3.5　Sources of information on the supply market, and individual suppliers, include: existing supplier records; suppliers' promotional information, catalogues, websites and sales representatives; relevant trade exhibitions; supplier visits; printed and online supplier or stockist directories (including directories of suppliers certified under quality standards); and recommendation by network contacts.

Schedules and lead times

3.6 The specification writer will need to know what the 'timeline' for the development and sourcing project is: when a potential supplier will need to be consulted; when final feedback from stakeholders will be gathered; when the specification will need to be signed off; when prototypes or samples will need to be ordered and delivered; when the requirement will be put up for quotation or tender, and the closing date for quotations or tenders to be received; when contracts or orders will need to be finalised; and – of course – when supplies will be required (in order to specify delivery dates).

3.7 The specification writer will need to gather information about:

- The deadline for delivery of the supplies, or commencement of the services (in consultation with users and operational plans)
- The lead time for ordering, production, testing, inspection and delivery of the supplies, or development and delivery of the services (in consultation with suppliers and logistics providers) – and therefore
- The latest date at which a purchase contract or order will need to be finalised.

3.8 A range of time line, scheduling and lead time information may be included in the specification (eg turn-around and response times).

Costs and budgetary constraints

3.9 Cost pressures and expenditure budgets are key constraints on specifications. If procurement's priority is to control or reduce costs, it may have to challenge users' tendency to customise and add variety, to over-specify features and quality, to minimise tolerances and/or to insist on swift response times, and to choose expensive branded models. All these things cost more, and in times of recession in particular, the priority may be to reduce costs at the expense of specified quality, speed, customisation and supplier flexibility.

3.10 The specification writer will need to know:

- The relative priority placed on cost reduction over quality and speed in a particular situation: a component may be critical, for example, or an order may be urgent, or the customer may be willing to pay more – in which case, cost may not be the most important factor in the specification.
- The expenditure budget set for the project. Budgets are, ideally, a genuine attempt to estimate costs in advance (plus contingency sums for overruns), in order to ensure that funds are available when needed. A 'bottom up' budgeting approach would aggregate estimates of costs for each of the inputs to the project, including an estimate of materials costs from the procurement department. A 'top down' approach would allocate a total sum (eg based on what the organisation can afford, or the cost of similar projects in the past, or a proportion of the estimated sales revenue or value added by the project), for allocation to different inputs. Budgets may be developed jointly by users, purchasers and the finance manager.
- Procurement objectives and targets for achieving reductions in sourcing, materials or service costs.
- Market prices for products and services, and where discounts can be obtained (eg by bulk procurement, early payment, negotiation with suppliers and so on)

- The likely ongoing or 'lifetime' costs of the proposed purchase: not just purchase price, but ownership costs such as insurance, maintenance, operating costs, consumables, disposal and so on.

Supplier processes

3.11 The processes used by potential suppliers to source, manufacture and deliver products or services are also important information for developing a specification.

- Suppliers' process capability and expertise may suggest opportunities for quality improvements or cost savings, which can be built into the specification.
- Shortcomings in suppliers' processes may create a risk that specified quality and service levels will not be able to be met consistently. This may affect the choice of supplier, or the extent of monitoring and inspection that will be required.
- Suppliers' processes may present compliance or reputational risk, in areas such as environmental manufacturing or corporate social responsibility. The specification may need to build in controls or improvement targets in regard to pollution, energy use or waste disposal, say, or the ethical treatment of employees. Otherwise, the buyer may find its own reputation damaged by association with the supplier.

4 Influences on specification development

4.1 A range of internal company policies and external legislation, regulation and standards may impact on the development of procurement specifications. Specification writers may have to take these factors into account – and specifications may also refer specifically to them, in order to identify minimum acceptable standards of practice or performance.

Company policy

4.2 The buying organisation may have a wide range of policies embracing areas such as:

- Its intention to comply with all relevant laws, regulations, standards, codes of practice and best practice benchmarks: these may be referred to in specifications
- Its aspirations for environmental sourcing and manufacture. For example, there may be recycling policies (dictating that recyclability and reverse logistics be built into specifications); policies for the minimisation of greenhouse gas (GHG) emissions (dictating that minimal non-renewable energy use be built into specifications); or sustainable supply policies (so that specifications require the use of sustainably managed raw materials, say).
- Its aspirations for corporate social responsibility and ethical trading. For example, specifications may require ethical sourcing of raw materials by suppliers, or ethical treatment of supplier employees (particularly in low-cost labour economies), or above-minimum standards of product health and safety.
- Sourcing policies, which may dictate that specifications are put up to tender, or are sufficiently 'open' to give opportunities to small or local suppliers, say, or whether the organisation favours early buyer involvement (EBI) and/or early supplier involvement (ESI).
- Quality, cost and pricing policies, which may dictate the relative priority given to quality, time and cost in specification decisions.

Other internal influences

4.3 In addition to policies, the process of specification development may be influenced by factors such as:

- *Organisation and management culture*: 'the way we do things round here'. Organisational values and customs may dictate whether a specification is collaborative or top-down; attitudes to quality and service; reliance on (or avoidance of) paperwork and bureaucracy – and so on.
- *Organisation structure*: this may influence the extent of cross-functional involvement in specification processes; whether decisions have to be referred upwards or are delegated to qualified staff; the status and role of procurement in the organisation; whether specification activity is centralised or devolved to user departments; and so on.
- *Budgets and budgetary controls* (as discussed above).

Legislation

4.4 Law and regulation places certain requirements on products and services which may need to be taken into account in developing specifications. Here are some examples.

- Quality standards and tolerances required to be *accredited* by relevant national and international quality standards, for instance for European products to receive the CE quality mark
- Quality standards and tolerances required for *product safety*, under relevant health and safety and consumer protection legislation and industry codes of practice (eg the strength, flexibility or weight-bearing capacity of construction materials; the chemical composition of materials to avoid health hazards; the restriction of ingredients such as additives in food products)
- Controls on the use, storage and transport of *substances and materials* which may be dangerous to health (eg chemicals, poisons, lead paint, asbestos, flammable or explosive materials, corrosive materials such as acids).
- *Environmental protection* law and regulation, dealing with issues such as the safe disposal or recyclability of waste and end-of-life products (including electrical and electronic waste and batteries).

4.5 Suppliers should be expected to be knowledgeable about, and compliant with, legislation relevant to their industry and products. However, the buyer is still liable in law if he incorporates outlawed materials or components in his products. One high-profile case study was the problems encountered by global toy company Mattel, which was forced to recall millions of toys, manufactured under licence in China, because the suppliers had purchased paint contaminated with US/EU-banned levels of lead, from unauthorised suppliers.

4.6 Buyers should therefore take proactive steps to:

- Draw the specification team's attention to known legal requirements
- Draw suppliers' attention to known legal requirements – especially if the law in the suppliers' country of operation is different from that of the buyer
- Implement their own compliance checks (audits, monitoring and inspection) on suppliers and supplies
- Use suppliers which are certified under quality and environmental standards, or encourage favoured suppliers to become so certified.

Stakeholders

4.7 Stakeholders are parties who have a legitimate interest in a process or plan, by virtue of the fact that they contribute to it, or are likely to be affected by it. As we have seen throughout this chapter, there are various internal stakeholders in the specification process (designers, users, marketing, finance, procurement), and various external stakeholders (suppliers, regulators, standards organisations, customers). Specifications are a tool of:

- *Stakeholder communication* and management: informing key stakeholders of what is required (suppliers) and what should be expected (users, finance, procurement)
- *Stakeholder marketing*: informing customers and regulators, for example, of the buying organisation's attention to quality, safety and environmental performance.

4.8 At the same time, it should be recognised that stakeholders often have different – and potentially divergent or competing – interests, and the process of specification may well highlight these. For example, marketers and customers will want the highest possible quality, features and performance – while finance and procurement professionals may want greater standardisation and cost control. Suppliers may want to drive the specification, getting the buyer to use what they offer – while buyers want to drive the specification, ensuring that suppliers supply what they require. Society as a whole, and pressure groups promoting particular causes, may want the highest possible ethical and environmental standards – but buyers and suppliers may need to be pragmatic, because of the higher costs of best practice in these areas.

5 The make/do or buy decision

Factors in make/do or buy decisions

5.1 The nature of the make/do or buy problem can be stated in fairly simple terms. At one extreme, a firm could make its products (or develop its services) entirely in-house, buying in perhaps nothing but raw materials: the value of the final product arises almost entirely from the work done by the firm. At the other extreme, a firm could minimise its own activities, buying in almost everything from outside suppliers (who would therefore be adding almost all the value in the finished product).

5.2 In most cases, of course, firms will occupy a middle position somewhere between these two extremes. This is the nature of the make/do or buy decision: where exactly should the firm position itself along this spectrum of possibilities? Where is the 'boundary of the firm'?

5.3 Make/do or buy decisions depend on a range of strategic and operational factors.

- The effects on total costs of production
- Profitability, risk and flexibility
- The availability of in-house competencies and capacity; how readily they can be acquired or expanded; and whether they will be consistently available in future. (Lack of adequate competence or capacity will push the firm towards the 'buy' end of the spectrum.)
- The availability of suitable external suppliers. A lack of suitable suppliers would push the firm towards the 'make/do' end of the spectrum.
- The need to retain knowledge and skill in-house for future applications.
- HR impacts. Will a decision to buy out lead to redundancies? Will a decision to make/do in-house lead to a need for training and/or recruitment?

5.4 Focus on core competencies has led many companies to buy in products, components or assemblies previously produced in-house, and to outsource a range of support functions (such as maintenance, catering, warehousing and transport, and staff recruitment and training) and even core functions such as sales and customer service (eg in call centres).

5.5 Broadly speaking, the advantages and disadvantages of strategic outsourcing can be summarised as in Table 5.1.

Table 5.1 *Advantages and disadvantages of strategic outsourcing*

ADVANTAGES OF STRATEGIC OUTSOURCING	DISADVANTAGES OF STRATEGIC OUTSOURCING
Support for downsizing: reduction in staffing, space and facilities costs	Costs of services and relationship and contract management
Allows focused investment of managerial, staff and other resources on core competencies	Loss of control and difficulties ensuring service standards
Leverages the specialist expertise, technologies, resources and economies of scale of suppliers, with potential to add more value at less cost than the organisation could achieve itself (for non-core activities)	Potential reputational damage if service or ethical issues arise
Enables synergy through collaborative supply relationships	Loss of in-house knowledge and competencies (for future needs)
	Loss of control over confidential information and intellectual property
	Ethical and employee relations issues of downsizing

5.6 Careful management is required to control the outsourced relationship, output and service quality, and ethical and employment standards – and their consequences for the outsourcing organisation and its brand.

The contribution of Procurement to make/do or buy decisions

5.7 Make/do or buy decisions require the input of many different functions *and* supply chain collaborators. The procurement and supply function may be particularly well placed to assess the implications of the 'buy' option, because it is familiar with: the supply market; supplier capabilities, capacity and compatibility; and likely comparative costs. It will also have a key role in the successful implementation and control of any outsourcing (buy) strategy, through supplier evaluation and selection, price negotiation, quality and service level specification, contracting, and ongoing contract and relationship management.

5.8 Here are some of the ways in which procurement can help.

- It encourages decision-making at a strategic (rather than purely operational) level, considering long-term objectives and impacts across the supply chain.
- It supports the use of Porter's 'value system' as a strategic framework, challenging each stage in the process from extraction of raw materials to purchase of the finished product by consumers to play its part in adding value.
- Managers are forced to take a broad view of the entire supply chain as a repository of skills and expertise. If a supplier has a greater ability to add value at low cost than in-house units, the buy option should be considered.
- Established supply chain relationships support decision-making: suppliers' capabilities will be known; a level of trust may have developed; information-sharing and relationship management systems may already be in place; and suppliers may be more likely to understand and support the firm's strategic goals.

Chapter summary

- Specifications often require cross-functional input from design and engineering, marketing, end users and procurement.
- Dobler and Burt identify four possible approaches to organising the specification process: early buyer involvement; formal committee approach; informal approach; and procurement co-ordinator approach.
- It adds risk to the process if the supplier is allowed to 'drive' the specification. It is preferable for the buyer to do this.
- Early buyer involvement and early supplier involvement can both improve the specification process.
- Cost pressures and expenditure budgets are key constraints on specifications. Procurement may have to challenge end-users' requirements in the interest of saving costs.
- Internal influences on specification development include company policy, organisation culture and organisation structure. External influences include legislation, quality standards, and the actions of stakeholders.
- An important decision at the corporate level is which activities to perform in house and which to outsource: the make/do or buy decision.

Self-test questions

Numbers in brackets refer to paragraphs where you can check your answers.

1. List characteristics of an effective specification. (1.5)

2. Describe the four possible approaches to organising the specification process, according to Dobler and Burt. (1.12)

3. List the contributions that procurement can make to specifications. (2.4–2.6)

4. What is the main purpose of ESI? (2.8)

5. Why are supplier processes an important piece of information in developing specifications? (3.11)

6. In what ways do legal and regulatory requirements impact on specifications? (4.4)

7. List advantages and disadvantages of strategic outsourcing. (Table 5.1)

CHAPTER 6

Creating Specifications

Assessment criteria and indicative content

2.2 Explain criteria that should be applied in creating specifications

- The importance of specifications in contracts with external customers and suppliers
- Creating specifications for products and services
- Conformance and output or outcome based approaches to developing specifications
- The role of key performance indicators (KPIs)

Section headings

1. Specifications and tolerances
2. The importance of specifications
3. Types of specification
4. Specifying services
5. The role of KPIs

Introduction

In this chapter we continue our discussion of specifications. We look in more detail at the different types of specification that you may come across. And we examine the particular difficulties of specifying services.

1 Specifications and tolerances

Tolerances

1.1 It is generally recognised that a supplier cannot match all the requirements of a specification exactly, all the time, so some room for variation is usually built into the specification. The term *tolerance* is used to describe a statement or measure of how much variation from specification will be acceptable, in the assessment of quality.

1.2 Tolerances will vary according to the nature of the work being specified. Consider a specification for an engineered component, for example: because such a component would have to fit within a complex assembly, and perform to a fine degree of accuracy, it would typically have an extremely small tolerance. The dimensions of such a component might be expressed as specification 'plus or minus' (+/−) 1 millimetre: if the specified dimension was 500mm, there would be leeway for the component to measure 499 or 501 millimetres.

1.3 Different sorts of tolerances might be set for services. A call centre might be required to answer incoming calls 'within five rings' (ie a tolerance of 1–5). A cleaning service might be required to have its employees on the premises and starting work 'between 7.00 pm and 7.30 pm' (ie a tolerance of 30 minutes).

The implications of zero defects

1.4 The concept of 'zero defects' (or 'get it right first time') is a cornerstone of radical quality management philosophies such as total quality management. It means, among other things, that a buyer relies on his suppliers to achieve 100% quality in their deliveries. This refers to all aspects of the buyer's orders: the supplier is expected to deliver exactly the right quantity, at exactly the right time and place, and exactly in line with the buyer's specification.

1.5 Zero defects has implications for:
- *Specifications*: exact requirements (defining right quality) will have to be set out, with very low or zero tolerance for variation, or for number of defects in an order
- *Supplier selection, evaluation and auditing*. Quality assurance staff from the buyer's organisation will check the supplier's capabilities to ensure that they are able to meet specification dependably
- *Quality control*: even if the supplier has been fully audited and certified, the buyer will still wish to inspect the first few deliveries to ensure that everything is working as it should be
- *Costs*, since the costs of assuring quality, or preventing defects, are generally less than the costs of poor quality
- The buyer's own *quality management*: the focus of zero defects is not just supplies from outside the organisation. Internal controls must work towards zero tolerance for defects in their own production processes, with the overall aim of delivering faultless product to the external customer.

1.6 In the present context, however, the main point about zero defects is that it builds quality in at the design stage of product development – in other words, as early as possible in the process. There is an old saying in information technology: 'garbage in, garbage out' (GIGO). The same applies to production processes. If defects are to be prevented (as opposed to detected once they have already occurred), it is necessary to get the inputs right – and accurate low-tolerance or zero-tolerance materials specifications are a key contributing factor.

1.7 So why wouldn't every specification provide for extremely small or zero tolerances, if the buyer knows exactly what he wants and sees the benefit of zero defects?
- Some work is difficult to specify accurately or prescriptively, so wider tolerances may be required within a 'looser' specification. This is often the case for service specifications, for example, as we will see later in the chapter.
- Tight tolerances are more costly to achieve, because of the more advanced machinery and skills required, extra time taken, and the cost of scrapping production that does not conform to specification.

2 The importance of specifications

The heart of the contract

2.1 Specifications are said to be 'the heart of the contract' between a buyer and seller, because contract law provides that:
- Goods supplied must conform to any specification of requirement included in the contract
- Goods supplied must be of *satisfactory quality* and *fit for their purpose* – mostly, clearly defined by specification.

2.2 A contract is formed when one party makes an 'offer' and the other party unconditionally 'accepts' it. A specification is part of the offer to buy, and if the supplier accepts the contract, it is contractually bound to fulfil the specification in full (within any specified tolerances).

2.3 In addition, under contract law, if a buyer tells a supplier the purpose for which a purchased item is to be used, the item delivered must effectively fulfil that purpose. A CIPS chief assessor uses the example of a bucket. If you specify a 5 litre bucket and the supplier delivers a 3 litre bucket, the item delivered is not fit for its purpose: it will not hold 5 litres of water. Adding to this example, if you tell the supplier that you want to use the bucket to hold a chemical (even if the bucket is usually used for water), and the supplier accepts the order, the bucket must be able to hold the chemical (without being eaten away etc) – otherwise it is not fit for its purpose.

2.4 An effective specification removes any doubt, ambiguity or misunderstanding in the supplier's mind as to what is required, and therefore what constitutes satisfactory quality and fitness for purpose.

Advantages and disadvantages of specifications

2.5 The main *advantages* claimed for using specifications are as follows.
- The process of drawing up specifications is a useful discipline. It forces careful consideration of needs and possible alternative ways of satisfying them. This can lead to other benefits, such as innovation and cost savings.
- If items are to be purchased from more than one source, the use of conformance specifications (specifying exactly what is to be supplied) may be essential to ensure uniformity.
- Specifications provide useful criteria for measuring the quality and acceptability of purchases once delivered.
- Specifications provide evidence, in the event of a dispute, as to what the purchaser required (and the supplier agreed to provide) as part of the contract.

2.6 The main *disadvantages* of using specifications are as follows.
- Detailed specification is an expensive and time consuming process, and almost certainly uneconomic for small-value purchases.
- The costs of inspection and quality control are greater than if simple specification (eg by brand name) is used.
- Specifications can become too firmly embedded: they need to be regularly reviewed, to ensure that the latest design decisions, and the latest developments in the supply market, are being taken into account.
- Specifications can create a temptation to over-specify, increasing cost (without necessarily adding value).

Consequences of poor specification

2.7 The consequences of ineffective specification processes are potentially costly for the organisation.
- There may be misunderstandings with suppliers over requirements and expectations (eg if the specification was vague, inaccurate or overly technical), leading to rejection of deliveries, lost production time, legal disputes and damaged supplier relationships.
- There may be misunderstandings with other stakeholders over requirements and expectations (eg if the specification did not take into account users' needs), leading to

internal conflict, resistance to use of the product and loss of credibility for procurement.
- There are more likely to be quality defects in the goods supplied, and, as we have seen, these are costly in terms of lost time, scrapped goods, rework, additional inspections and controls, and so on. If defects reach the customer, there may be additional serious consequences of lost customer loyalty, lost business, the adjustment of complaints and so on.
- Poorly defined specifications may mean that, even if the materials conform to specification, they will fail to function as they should. The risk and cost of such a failure is borne by the buyer.
- Goods and services may be over-specified: related to some 'ideal' standard, without reference to users' actual needs, the cost of higher standards, or the added value actually contributed by higher standards.

3 Types of specification

Conformance and performance specifications

3.1 Two main categories of specification are conformance specifications (or design specifications) and performance specifications (or functional specifications). You need to be able to distinguish clearly between the two.

- With a *conformance* specification, the buyer details exactly what the required product, part or material must consist of. This may take the form of an engineering drawing or blueprint, a chemical formula or 'recipe' of ingredients, or a sample of the product to be duplicated. The supplier may not know in detail, or even at all, what function the product will play in the buyer's manufacturing. It is his task simply to *conform to the description* provided by the buyer.
- With a *performance (functional)* specification, the buyer describes what he expects the part or material to be able to achieve, in terms of the functions it will perform and the level of performance it should reach. It is up to the supplier to supply a product which will *satisfy these requirements*: the buyer specifies the 'ends', and the supplier has relatively flexibility as to 'means' of achieving those ends. (Your syllabus refers to this type of specification in the phrase 'output or outcome based approaches').

3.2 Conformance specifications are becoming less common, for a number of reasons.

- It can be very difficult, time-consuming and costly to draft a comprehensive description of exactly what is wanted.
- The buyer bears the risk of the design not performing. Suppliers who conform to the letter of the description are safeguarded in law, even if the product supplied does not perform its intended function.
- Conformance specifications may restrict the potential supplier base. A tight specification may be capable of fulfilment only by a small number of suppliers. In effect, the capabilities of other potential suppliers have been 'specified away'.
- The prescriptive nature of the specification may restrict innovation and the range of solutions to problems. This is a particular problem if the specification details the *means* by which the supplied items should be manufactured: the buyer potentially closes himself off from manufacturing developments of which he may be unaware – especially in supply markets where technology is developing quickly. In addition, the buyer may be ignoring 'off-the-shelf' solutions to the requirement, and incurring unnecessary costs for a 'bespoke' solution.

3.3 However, we will look at a number of methods of conformance specification, before turning our attention to performance specifications.

Technical or design specifications

3.4 A technical specification or design specification may take the form of engineering drawings, designs or blueprints, or detailed descriptions. Such a specification is a highly prescriptive written specification or drawing giving a fully detailed definition of what is required. A technical specification would typically include aspects such as the following.

- The scope of the specification (its objectives and content)
- Definitions: explanation of any technical or specialised terms used
- The purpose of the equipment or material that is the subject of the specification
- Reference to related documents (such as standards or legislation) which apply
- Materials requirements (including approved or excluded materials), properties (eg dimensions, strength), tolerances and permissible variability
- Appearance, texture and finish requirements of the finished product, including identification marks, operating symbols, safety instructions and so on
- Drawings, samples or models of the required product (where available)
- Conditions under which the item or material is to be installed, used, manufactured or stored
- Maintenance and reliability requirements
- Specification of packaging (including any special conditions in transit) and protection
- Information to be provided by the supplier for users, such as instructions, or advice on installation, operation and maintenance.

3.5 Designs, technical drawings and blueprints are commonly used in engineering and construction or architecture environments, which require a high degree of technical accuracy and very low tolerances (because of the complexity of assembly and machine function). They have the following advantages.

- Allowing a large amount of technically precise and detailed information to be conveyed
- Supporting fair competition between suppliers, since the same plans can be sent to a number of potential suppliers for quotation
- Offering a precise standard against which deliveries can be measured, by comparison with the detailed technical specifications
- Minimising risk, and taking best advantage of situations in which the buying organisation has more design or technical expertise than prospective suppliers.

3.6 The *disadvantages* of design specification are those identified for conformance specifications in general. In particular, engineering drawings and blueprints are time-consuming and costly to produce, with a need for highly-qualified professional input.

Specification by chemical/physical properties

3.7 'Composition' specifications are the equivalent of technical specifications for different types of product, such as chemicals and manufactured materials (such as plastics), engineering or construction: they specify the chemical or physical make-up required. This may be particularly important where:

- Certain physical properties (eg strength, flexibility, durability) are important for safety and/ or performance. So, for example, the metal used in car manufacture must have certain properties of shock absorption or crumpling, for safety purposes.
- Certain materials are restricted by law, regulation or codes of practice, for health, safety or environmental reasons. Examples include some of the heavy metals in batteries, lead in paint, non-recyclable packing and so on.

3.8 The advantages and disadvantages of composition specifications are similar to those of technical specifications.

Specification by brand name

3.9 A buyer may specify what he requires by means of a brand name. If you are familiar with a particular product on the market, and it meets your criteria, you can simply order the required quantity of that brand, usually supported by a particular model name or number.

3.10 There are some *advantages* to this approach.
- It is simple, quick, easy and cheap to administer. Provided the buyer is satisfied that the specified brand or model will fulfil the requirement, he can simply order it by name and there is no ambiguity about what he will receive. This may be important if the quantities required, or their total value, do not justify a costly specification process – which is why the method is common in small business and consumer purchases.
- Branded products will tend to be of good quality and consistency. The manufacturer will have invested heavily in building up the brand name and will protect its value by doing everything possible to ensure that customers are satisfied – which implies concentrated attention to quality issues.
- Branded products should be easy to source, since, again, the manufacturer will have invested in building up the brand and will therefore ensure that it is readily accessible to the market.
- If the brand is well known, it may be a selling point when the buyer's own product is finished and offered for sale. One well-known example is the use of Intel microprocessors in computers: 'Intel inside' is a point of appeal to customers, and may even be demanded by them.
- Procurement by brand name may be essential if a particular part or material is patented.

3.11 However, there are also *disadvantages* to this approach.
- For the very reasons already mentioned – high quality, reliability, well known name and image – branded items are often more expensive than unbranded equivalents.
- There may be restricted choice of branded products in a market, and perhaps only one supplier for a given product.
- The supplier may alter the specification of its product, without changing the branding or notifying customers. Ordering by brand alone may not therefore conform to the requirement.
- Branded products may be 'fakes' (products of low quality passed off under the brand name), and generic products claimed as identical equivalents to branded products (common in the pharmaceuticals industry, for example) may not be genuinely identical. This may be a particular hazard in consumer purchases.
- Manufacturers may tend to assume, without proper testing, that branded materials or components will be satisfactory, but cutting corners on quality assurance is always a risk.

Specification by sample

3.12 If the purchaser knows exactly what he wants, because he already has some, he can send a sample to the supplier, requiring him simply to duplicate the features and performance of the sample. It is also common in some industries for suppliers to provide samples (eg the swatches of materials provided by upholsterers, and sample pots of paints provided by paint manufacturers). The buyer can then simply specify the model to be duplicated.

3.13　The main advantages of a sampling approach are as follows.

- If a buyer relies on a sample provided by the supplier, it is legally entitled to receive goods which correspond with the sample.
- Some samples can be used or tested to assess suitability, prior to purchase.
- They are a quick and easy method of specifying requirements, without having to describe features in detail.
- If a supplier is asked to produce a sample, the buyer can be assured that he has developed the required production methods to do so in future.

3.14　The main disadvantage of specification by sample is that it may be difficult to measure the product supplied against the sample. Is it really the same, other than in obvious observable measures such as colour or size? If deeper testing is required to establish the product's compliance with criteria such as chemical composition, strength, flexibility, functionality and so on, it might be preferable to specify those characteristics. Also, it is necessary to have some assurance that a good quality sample is not merely a 'one off', done to secure the order: the supplier must be able to produce the same quality dependably.

Specification by market grade

3.15　Some materials, especially commodities such as steel and wool, are subject to a grading system, in which qualities such as purity, strength or flexibility are standardised. Buyers in the relevant industries are familiar with what is implied by each grade and can specify what they want simply by ordering '1,000 tonnes of Grade X'.

3.16　This has the virtue of simplicity and wide acceptance within an industry, but it does not necessarily specify the full range of parameters that may be relevant to a purchase.

Specification by standards

3.17　Standards are documents that stipulate or recommend minimum levels of performance and quality of goods and services. Like market grades, they offer a 'short-hand' method of specifying common requirements for common products and services – and for the processes used in their production and delivery (eg environmental management and quality management). The buyer can simply specify that supplies be compliant with a given standard, or that the supplier's processes be accredited under a given standard scheme.

3.18　Standards may relate to various aspects of product quality.

- *Standard terms and symbols* (harmonising the 'language' used in specification: there are over 100 ISO standards, for example, which use specific conventions for technical drawings)
- The *dimensions* of items (encouraging interchangeability and variety reduction)
- The *performance or safety requirements* of items, with acceptable tolerances
- Environmental requirements (eg on pollution control or waste disposal)
- *Codes of practice*, giving guidance on best practice in relation to engineering and construction techniques, installation, maintenance, provision of services and so on
- *Methods of testing*, as a standard way of measuring the values of product characteristics and behavioural standards.

3.19　Standards are produced at different levels and by different bodies.

- Company standards and codes of practice, setting out standard specifications and tolerances

for a range of bought-out items, can be produced by various functions as a guide to design, procurement, manufacturing and marketing operations.
- Trade or industry standards are produced by trade associations and professional bodies.
- National standards, such as those produced by the **British Standards Institution (BSI)**. The BSI also offers independent quality assessment and certification for firms, under its Kitemark, Safety Mark, Registered Firms and Registered Stockist schemes.
- International standards, such as those produced by the **International Standards Organisation (ISO)** or the European Committee for Standardisation (CEN) in Western Europe. You may be familiar with the ISO 9000 series of standards on quality management systems, for example, or ISO 14001 on environmental management systems.

3.20 Lysons & Farrington urge procurement staff to be aware of the major trade, national and international standards applicable to their industry and the items they buy regularly. The *advantages* of using standards are as follows.

- Clear specifications, no uncertainty or ambiguity as to requirement – and therefore less potential for error and conflict with suppliers
- Saving of the time and cost of preparing company specifications and related explanations and discussions
- Reduced time-to-market of finished product, because of reduced design time
- Accurate comparison of quotations, since all potential suppliers are quoting on the same specifications
- A wider range of potential suppliers, and less reliance on (more costly) specialist suppliers, because of the general application of the standard
- Saving of inventory and purchase costs, as a result of standardisation (in the sense of 'variety reduction'). The organisation may, where possible, use 'generic' or standard items instead of multiple lines of own-design or variant items. This should reduce stock holding, and enable the aggregation of orders (rather than multiple small orders of variant items), for bulk discounts and reduced transaction and materials handling costs.

3.21 The main *disadvantage* of using standards, however, is that – like any generic specification – they may not accurately reflect the buyer's requirements. They may also fail to reflect the very latest technology or practices, since it takes some years for standards to be developed and updated. Full harmonisation of standards internationally has not yet been achieved, so there may be complexities in using British or European standards in Asia, for example.

Performance specification

3.22 A performance or **functional specification** is a relatively brief document (compared to a conformance specification) that defines the functionality or performance to be achieved, and details of key input parameters. It does *not* (unlike a conformance specification) prescribe how the functionality or performance is to be achieved (in terms of materials, designs and processes).

3.23 A performance specification would typically include the following details.

- The functionality, performance or capabilities to be achieved, within specified tolerances
- Key process inputs which will contribute to performance, including available utilities (electricity, solar power and so on)
- The operating environment and conditions in which the performance is to be achieved (and extreme or unusual conditions in which it is not expected)

- How the product is required to interface with other elements of the process
- Required quality levels (including relevant standards)
- Required safety levels and controls (including relevant standards)
- Required environmental performance levels and controls (including relevant standards)
- Criteria and methods to be used to measure whether the desired function has been achieved.

3.24 There are a number of advantages to such an approach, which have made performance specifications increasingly common.

- Performance specifications are easier and cheaper to draft, compared to a more detailed, prescriptive (conformance) approach.
- The efficacy of the specification does not depend on the technical knowledge of the buyer. Suppliers may well know better than the buyer what is required, and how it can best be manufactured.
- Suppliers can use their full expertise, technologies and innovative capacity to develop optimum, lowest-cost solutions.
- A greater share of specification risk is borne by the supplier. If the part supplied does not perform its function, the buyer is entitled to redress (whereas, with a conformance specification, the specifier bears responsibility for the functionality of the finished result).
- The potential supply base is wider than with a conformance specification. If the task is to supply something – anything – that will perform a particular function, the expertise of different suppliers could potentially provide a wide range of solutions.

3.25 It is particularly appropriate to use performance specifications in the following circumstances.

- Suppliers have greater relevant technical and manufacturing expertise than the buyer – so that the best knowledge is being used and leveraged. It should also be noted that the buyer will be highly reliant on the supplier's expertise: this puts pressure on supplier selection and evaluation.
- Technology is changing rapidly in the supplying industry – so that the buyer is not in a position of specifying yesterday's methodologies, but gets the best out of suppliers' innovation capacity and technological development.
- There are clear criteria for evaluating alternative solutions put forward by suppliers competing for the contract. These should be clearly communicated to potential suppliers, who may invest considerable time and resources in coming up with proposals, and will want to be assured that the selection process is fair.
- The buyer has sufficient time and expertise to assess the potential functionality of suppliers' proposals and competing alternatives (particularly if the supplier is using technology with which the buyer is unfamiliar). The complexity of the evaluation process is the major disadvantage of the performance specification approach.

4 Specifying services

4.1 It is harder to draft accurate specifications for services than for goods, because of their intangible nature – and yet this makes it even more important, otherwise buyer and supplier could argue interminably as to whether the service was exactly what was asked for, or of an adequate standard. An advertising agency or architect might submit a design which meets all the client's stated criteria in regard to aims, inclusions, style and budget – but the client may still find it is not what he wanted. Who, if anyone, is at fault – and who pays for the second attempt?

4.2 The more work that can be done at the pre-contract stage, the better. This means agreeing service levels, schedules and the basis for charges in as much detail as possible before the contract is signed: disputes often stem from differing expectations on the part of buyer and supplier.

4.3 This is particularly vital if the organisation is outsourcing service functions currently performed by in-house staff. The organisation will typically seek to close down its internal service provision, disposing of equipment, redeploying or shedding staff and so on. Once this has been done, the supplier is in a strong position – and shouldn't be given the opportunity to renegotiate the contract on the basis that the original agreement was vague on details of the service to be offered.

4.4 The specification of services requires professional procurement input, but it is equally important to involve user and beneficiary departments. For one thing, they are ideally placed (as customers) to help determine the level of service they require or expect; for another, involvement will help to secure 'buy in' and minimise later disputes.

4.5 **Supplier management** is also an important ingredient in successful service buying. Often the level of service agreed upon is expressed in terms which are difficult to measure. It is not like purchasing steel rods, which indisputably are – or are not – of the diameter or length specified. It is vital that from the earliest stages, the supplier is made aware of exactly what the buyer regards as satisfactory performance and exactly what will be regarded as unsatisfactory. This is where service level agreements come in (as we saw in Chapter 1).

5 The role of KPIs

Key performance indicators

5.1 In recent years, organisational performance measurement and the associated metrics (ie performance measures) have received much focus from academics and business practitioners. The role of these measures is important in supporting business management at strategic, tactical and operational levels of the business.

5.2 It is therefore not surprising that supplier performance measurement is being used increasingly to assist organisations in their search for competitive advantage in today's business environments. The following section examines how performance measures can be developed and used to support supplier improvement initiatives.

5.3 Key performance indicators (KPIs) are measurements used in business to quantify objectives so as to reflect the strategic performance of an organisation. These measurements can be both financial and non-financial in nature. They provide focus on the achievement of outcomes critical to the current and future success of an organisation.

5.4 There is no magic blueprint for the formulation and application of KPIs because clearly they will vary considerably from business to business depending on the nature of the organisation and its overall strategic aims. It is crucial that any developed KPIs are aligned to overall corporate objectives.

5.5 What makes a good KPI? The answer to this question is frequently expressed in terms of the acronym **SMART**. A KPI is SMART if it is:

- Specific
- Measurable
- Agreed /achievable
- Realistic
- Time-bounded (ie there must be a time specified within which the objective is to be achieved)

5.6 However, these criteria do not address the issue of corporate alignment – aligning of functional objectives with overall corporate objectives. In response to this, the **SMARTA** approach is being increasingly encouraged – the additional 'A' relates to the KPI **alignment** with corporate objectives.

KPI classification

5.7 KPIs can be categorised as either quantitative (fact-based measurements), or qualitative ('softer', more subjective measures, developed mostly from semi-structured sources such as customer surveys).

5.8 The traditional approach to using KPIs has been based on quantitative measurement. However, with the increasing focus on non-manufacturing sectors more judgmental approaches of measurement are also required in the assessment of issues such as quality of care provision.

5.9 Another classification of KPIs distinguishes between strategic and operational considerations. Having established the corporate strategic positioning, KPIs are developed to reflect these objectives. The following stage is to convert this strategic intent into operational initiatives for which associated KPIs are developed in turn. The critical issue here is that there is a direct alignment between strategic and operational KPIs. Should they become 'decoupled' this will lead to potential strategic disappointment and business frustration.

KPIs and improving supplier performance

5.10 Companies have traditionally measured direct suppliers' performance in order to control quality, reduce costs and ensure timely performance. This approach has been practised more actively in certain sectors than others. For example, the automotive sector has historically applied supplier rating systems and performance indices in order to improve supplier performance and subsequently to gain competitive advantage in global markets.

5.11 Supplier KPIs can be viewed as a mechanism by which a supplier's value to the organisation can be assessed. For example, they can be used to assess the supplier's performance in the light of the company's requirements in relation to the total cost of the goods or services purchased from the supplier.

5.12 Using KPIs to measure performance can enable the following activities.

- Support a clear long-term objective for each party (provided appropriate KPIs are established)
- Measure performance and establish associated improvement targets
- Manage supplier improvement programmes
- Strengthen and improve supplier relations by bringing mutual benefits to both parties
- Assist in developing suppliers
- Reward performance achievement
- Justify continued trading with the current supplier
- Alternatively, identify the need to find a new supplier
- Drive continuous improvement

5.13 The old saying 'what gets measured, gets managed' is very relevant to management in general and in particular to the procurement function. These key diagnostic measures are critical to inform and guide any corrective action related to the major input mechanism into the business.

Development and measurement of supplier KPIs

5.14 To achieve consistent performance in delivery, price, quality etc requires diligence and consistency together with a logically developed approach to establishing supplier KPIs. The following paragraphs outline some of the key stages in developing appropriate KPIs.

5.15 It is critical to align any supplier measurement with procurement objectives, which in turn must be aligned with corporate goals. For example, the supplier focus can be centred on cost of quality, responsiveness etc but the subsequent priority weighting needs to directly reflect the procurement department objectives.

5.16 Improvement of long-term supplier performance comes about through a clear, easy to understand measurement scoreboard with just a few KPIs. We should minimise the number of measurements because it is important that the performance measurement programme is easily understood by the suppliers. We should choose a few key areas such as delivery, quality etc and display them for all suppliers to see. We then measure KPIs frequently, and actively visualise the results via feedback mechanisms to the supplier (eg online access to updated scorecards).

5.17 Measurements must be easy to calculate and explain (data collection and the subsequent analysis is a costly process). In addition to the traditional quantitative measurements, buyers should also consider using some qualitative survey findings as well. Finally, we should develop an overall supplier rating which will give the added advantage of comparing one company with another.

5.18 Effective communication is also important. We should explain to the supplier exactly the performance standard expected. If possible, we should develop individual requirements for each supplier, rather than using more general criteria. Buyers should issue recent history trend data (if available) with a written explanation of key issues and requirements related to the individual supplier.

5.19 Whenever possible, buyers should involve suppliers in developing the performance measurement programme; suppliers can sometimes contribute valuable experiences from their other customers.

Chapter summary

- The role of a specification is to define the requirement and to communicate it clearly to suppliers.
- Modern thinking on quality emphasises the concept of zero defects.
- Specifications are usually a key element in the contract between buyer and supplier.
- In a conformance specification the buyer details exactly what he wants and it is the supplier's task to provide it. In a performance specification the buyer details what he wants the product to do, and the supplier has flexibility in what he provides to achieve that objective.
- There are numerous ways in which a specification may be made: by chemical or physical properties, by brand name, by sample, by market grade, by standards etc.
- There are particular difficulties in preparing specifications for services, mostly because a service is intangible.
- It is important to monitor the performance of suppliers. Appropriate KPIs must be devised to achieve this.

Self-test questions

Numbers in brackets refer to paragraphs where you can check your answers.

1. What is meant by tolerances? (1.1)
2. Explain the implications of the zero defects concept. (1.5)
3. List advantages and disadvantages of using specifications. (2.5, 2.6)
4. What are the consequences of poor specification? (2.7)
5. Why are conformance specifications becoming less common? (3.2)
6. List advantages and disadvantages of specifying by brand name. (3.10, 3.11)
7. List advantages of referring to published standards in specifications. (3.20)
8. When might it be appropriate to use performance specifications? (3.25)
9. What is meant by a SMART KPI? (5.5)

CHAPTER 7
Sourcing and Selecting Suppliers

Assessment criteria and indicative content

2.3 Assess approaches to the sourcing of supplies
- Surveying the market
- Supplier appraisal
- Measuring supplier performance

Section headings

1. Surveying the market
2. Criteria for supplier appraisal
3. Information for supplier appraisal
4. Measuring supplier performance

Introduction

This chapter focuses on the one area of the procurement cycle that has not substantially been addressed by earlier learning outcomes: that is, the sourcing (identification) and selection of suppliers.

This is important enough to be considered the 'sixth right of procurement' by some authors. In other words, the aim of procurement is to secure delivery of the right quality goods in the right quantity to the right place at the right time, and at the right price – from the 'right supplier'. In a sense, though, this is implied by the five rights themselves, because you won't get the right quality, quantity, delivery service or price from the wrong supplier.

1 Surveying the market

1.1 Not every purchase decision requires the location and selection of new sources of supply. As Baily et al summarise the matter:

'The buyer would check first if there is already some commitment by long-term contract, in which case an order could be placed immediately. In the absence of such agreement, the buyer would ask if there is an existing source of supply whose performance is satisfactory; if so, the usual practice is to reorder from that source unless there is reason to review the position. Reasons for reviewing the position include price increase request, failure to meet specification, unsatisfactory performance as demonstrated by vendor ratings, internal pressure to save money, or simply that some time has elapsed since the position was last reviewed.'

1.2 There may, however, be the need to source a new product or service – or the buyer may simply wish to stay aware of potential alternative providers in the supply market, if requirements (or existing suppliers' performance) change, or if opportunities arise to investigate better-value or more innovative solutions.

Sources of information on potential suppliers

1.3 A number of sources of information may be consulted to identify and research potentially suitable suppliers.

- The buyer's own *database of existing and past suppliers*, including records of their offerings, performance evaluations and so on (discussed in more detail below). This may be supplemented by the buyer's lists of preferred, approved or authorised suppliers, indicating which suppliers have been pre-qualified for use.
- The *marketing communications* of potential suppliers: advertising, direct mail, brochures and catalogues, visits from sales representatives, websites and so on. Catalogues (and their electronic equivalents) may be particularly helpful, with detailed product descriptions, trading terms, price lists and so on.
- *Internet* search for websites including business directories and listings, searchable databases designed to promote exports and specialist procurement resources.
- *Online market exchanges*, auction sites and supplier/buyer forums, which may also allow the posting of requests for quotation and other exchanges.
- *Published general directories* (eg Yellow Pages) and specialist trade and industry registers and directories of suppliers and stockists. Trade directories (eg published by Dun & Bradstreet) provide information about suppliers' products or services and may also include analysis or rating of the firm's capabilities or financial profile.
- The *general and trade or industry press* (newspapers, magazines, journals and bulletins) and specialist procurement journals (such as *Supply Management*) which may carry news and feature articles, supplier advertising, listings, statistical digests and so on.
- *Trade fairs, exhibitions and conferences*, which may provide opportunities for visitors to view competing products and prototypes, meet supplier representatives and contacts, discuss supplier offerings and buyer requirements, and gather relevant literature for the catalogue file. This can often be cost-effective research, since a number of suppliers are present in one place, and appointments can be made in advance to maximise the use of the time. However, there may also be costs to attending exhibitions, particularly if they are overseas.
- *Organisations promoting trade*, such as trade associations, embassies, chambers of commerce, export associations and so on – and their websites.
- *Informal networking* and information exchange with colleagues and other procurement professionals (eg recommendations and referrals from other buyers, word of mouth about suppliers' reputations)

Information in a supplier database

1.4 Once an organisation has an established supply base, it will usually store information about existing, past and potential suppliers in a *supplier database* or procurement information system. This might include a range of information: Table 7.1.

Table 7.1 *Supplier information database*

INFORMATION ABOUT EXISTING SUPPLIERS	SOURCES OF INFORMATION
Contact details (including details of account managers, where relevant)	Trade registers and directories, trade and industry exhibitions and conferences
Products and services offered	Supplier literature, websites, corporate reports and accounts
Standard or negotiated terms and conditions of trade, including prices, rates or fees where known	Supplier sales and customer service staff
Approved or preferred status of supplier	Feedback from own staff, vendor managers etc
Average value and frequency of spend with each existing supplier (used to identify key accounts)	Contract and transaction files and records
Special capabilities (eg late customisation capability, EDI) suggesting supplier selection when special needs arise	Reported financial and operational results (eg cost reductions, new product development, lead times)
Results of supplier appraisals, audits and ratings	Supplier appraisal, audit and rating reports
Vendor performance history: quality, lead times, delivery, compliance, disputes	Testimonials or reports from other customers (eg by request or business networking)
Current systems, framework agreements and call-off contracts in place	Electronic performance monitoring (eg goods inwards tracking)

Supplier appraisal

1.5 Having 'surveyed the market' and identified firms that are (theoretically) in the business of supplying the goods or services required, the buyer may choose to find out more about some of the suppliers who are potentially most suitable. Some of this additional 'qualifying' information may be built into the original supply market survey, as outlined earlier. However, the buyer may not have been able to gather substantial information about a supplier – or may only have gathered unsubstantiated information: that is, suppliers' claims about themselves (which, as marketing communication, cannot be taken at face value) or the subjective opinions of third parties (which may, likewise, not be entirely accurate or relevant to the buyer's needs).

1.6 A formal, systematic approach to information gathering about the supplier may be required. This is variously known as 'supplier appraisal', 'supplier evaluation', 'supplier quality assessment' or 'supplier pre-qualification'.

2 Criteria for supplier appraisal

Why pre-qualify suppliers?

2.1 The purpose of supplier appraisal, evaluation or pre-qualification is to ensure that a potential supplier will be able to perform any contract or tender that it is awarded, to the required standard.

2.2 This avoids the risk of later problems in the tender or negotiation process. The buyer does not want the wasted cost, time, effort and embarrassment of awarding a contract (on the basis of lowest price) to a tenderer who *subsequently* turns out to lack capacity or technical capability to handle the work, or turns out to have systems and values that are incompatible with the buying organisation, or turns out to be financially unstable and unable to complete the work because of cashflow problems or business failure.

2.3 In addition, having a list of pre-qualified suppliers reduces the investigations needed for individual tenders and purchases: the buyer already knows that any supplier on the approved list has been assessed as capable of fulfilling requirements. This may be particularly helpful where routine procurement activity is devolved to user department buyers, who may not have the expertise to evaluate or select new suppliers for themselves. Instead, they can choose from a list of suppliers pre-assessed and qualified by procurement specialists.

2.4 A full-scale supplier appraisal exercise is time-consuming and costly, so it may not be required for all new suppliers (eg for one-off, standardised or low-value purchases). It will be particularly important, however, for strategic or non-standard items; for major high-value purchases (eg capital equipment); for potential long-term supply partnerships; and for international sourcing and outsourcing (because of the risks involved).

Criteria for supplier evaluation or appraisal

2.5 A supplier appraisal may cover a wide and complex variety of factors that a buyer may consider essential or desirable in its suppliers. What to appraise is related to the requirements of the particular purchaser and purchase type, but all appraisals should evaluate factors such as the following.

- Financial status and stability
- Capacity of the company to produce
- Technical capability
- Environmental management systems and ISO14000
- Quality management systems and ISO9000
- Corporate social responsibility (CSR)
- Conformance to legislation
- The supplier's supply chain
- The supplier's customer base
- The culture of the company
- The identified costs of the proposed purchase

2.6 **Financial status and stability** refer to the supplier's profitability, its cashflow position (whether it has working funds to pay its bills, buy materials and pay workers), the assets it owns, the debts it owes, how its costs are structured and allocated, and so its overall financial 'health'. These factors will reflect on the ability of the supplier to fulfil its contract with the buyer. They may raise the risk of delivery or quality problems – and more drastic disruption to supply (and complex legal issues) if the supplier's business fails and it becomes insolvent. They will also impact on the prices the supplier will be able to charge the buyer.

2.7 **Capacity to produce** and **technical capability** refer to factors in the supplier's operational capacity and facilities, such as the following.

- Whether it produces (or can produce) the kinds of items, or deliver the kinds of services, required
- How much volume the supplier will be able to handle (its production capacity)
- What engineering, innovation and design capability it has (where relevant)
- What type of plant and machinery it has, and whether it is capable of producing items within the tolerances set by the buyer's specification
- How old and how well maintained the plant and machinery is, reflecting the risk of production 'down time' if machinery breaks down or wears out

- The efficiency of factory layout and processes (which will impact on productivity and also cost)

2.8 Capacity and capability may also be assessed with reference to:

- The *human resources* of the supplying organisation. A supplier appraisal may take into account the skills of the supplier's workforce; the ability and drive of its management; employee morale and motivation (which may impact on productivity or quality of work); the health of employee relations (which may reduce or increase the risk of industrial action, say); and whether there is a dependable supply of labour in the area (since skill shortages may affect production or raise costs).
- *Organisation structure*. How clear is accountability for performance? Will the supplier be able to respond flexibly to the buyer's demands and changing circumstances (eg with good cross-functional communication and versatile teams)? Does it operate account or contract management for ongoing contact with the buyer?
- *Performance*: the supplier's track record, the buyer's own vendor rating of the supplier (where available), reports and evidence of previous completed projects, customer testimonials and so on.

2.9 **Adherence to systems and procedures** may embrace a number of criteria.

- *Compatibility* of the supplier's systems and procedures with those of the buyer (or its ability and willingness to adapt to the buyer's requirements)
- Willingness of the supplier to comply with any procedures, rules or systems required by the buyer. Examples include: development of a quality management system per ISO9000 or an environmental management system per ISO14000; third party monitoring of the supplier's labour management practices (particularly in low-cost labour economies); protocols for the protection of confidential information and intellectual property; sound capacity planning and production control – and so on.
- *Quality management systems*: the supplier's standards accreditation (if any); its quality management methods (ideally based on quality assurance, not just quality control); its awareness of and willingness to adopt total quality management principles (eg aspiration for 'zero defects', involvement of employees in quality issues); its willingness to commit to continuous improvement programmes
- *IT development*: the potential for e-business and systems integration with the supplier, for more efficient procurement processes (eg whether the supplier is connected to EDI, or willing to be so; whether the supplier uses technology to enable electronic tracking of deliveries and inventory and so on).

2.10 You are unlikely to need to know very much detail on ISO9000 or ISO14000, so here is a brief summary.

2.11 **ISO9000** is a group of quality management standards laid down by the International Organisation for Standardisation (ISO). The standards are 'built around business processes, with a strong emphasis on improvement and a focus on meeting the needs of customers'. They are generic and adaptable to all kinds of organisations. The current series includes the following standards.

- ISO9000: Quality Management Systems: Fundamentals and Vocabulary
- ISO9001: Quality Management Systems: Requirements
- ISO9004: Guidelines for Performance Improvement

2.12 The ISO9000 standard identifies quality management systems as comprising four main processes.

- Management responsibility (management commitment, customer focus, quality policy setting, planning, accountability, communication and review)
- Resource management (provision of resources, human resources, infrastructure and work environment to support quality)
- Product realisation (customer research, product design and/or development, procurement, production and service operations)
- Measurement, analysis and improvement (monitoring and measurement of performance, control of non-conforming product, analysis of data, and improvement planning)

2.13 **ISO14000** is an equivalent series of international standards focusing on environmental management systems (EMS). An EMS gives an organisation a systematic process for assessing and managing its impact on the environment. The standard is designed to help develop such a system, as well as providing a supporting audit and review programme.

2.14 The major requirements for an EMS under ISO14001 include the following.

- An environmental policy statement, including commitment to prevent pollution, improve environmental performance, and comply with all legal requirements
- Identification of all aspects of the organisation's activities that could impact on the environment
- Performance objectives and targets for environmental performance
- Implementation of an EMS to meet those objectives and targets, including employee training, instructions, procedures etc
- Periodic auditing and review, with corrective and preventive action taken where necessary

2.15 **Corporate social responsibility** (CSR): a buyer may want to pre-qualify a supplier on the basis of CSR:

- To support the buyer's own CSR objectives
- To minimise the risk of reputational damage (and costs) arising from being associated with an unethical or irresponsible supplier.

2.16 **Conformance to legislation,** or 'compliance', may be part of a wider assessment of environmental and ethical considerations: the supplier's compliance record (on workplace healthy and safety, product safety and labelling, environmental protection and so on), and its stated policies and values in these areas. A non-compliant supplier may create a risk of non-compliance in the buyer's products, laying it open to product recalls and/or legal action. A supplier attracting publicity for unethical or environmentally damaging practices may equally be a source of reputational risk for the buyer, because of its association with the supplier.

2.17 The **supplier's supply chain** should be looked at as:

- A supporting factor in its capacity to produce and its technical capability. Can the supplier dependably access the materials, services, expertise and extra capacity it may require to fulfil the contract, from its own suppliers? How well managed is the supply chain, and the relationships with suppliers: will it support high quality, reliable delivery, flexibility (eg for just in time supply or late customisation) and innovation?
- A supporting factor in its legal, ethical and environmental compliance – and in the management of reputational risk to the buyer. There is increasing pressure for organisations to be aware of (and indirectly responsible for) the practices of their whole supply chains.

2.18 The **supplier's customer base** will also be relevant for various reasons.

- The buyer may be reassured of the supplier's quality by a customer base including large, reputable and 'blue-chip' clients, particularly if it can approach some of these for references or testimonials about the supplier's performance.
- The supplier's current 'order book' will indicate whether its goods or services are in demand – or whether (for reasons that may need investigating) business is slow.
- The customer base will also indicate whether the supplier's output is relevant to the buyer's industry and requirements, eg if the supplier's customers have similar business processes, technology, products, market position or expenditure budgets to the buyer.
- An additional consideration will be whether the supplier's customer base includes the buyer's direct competitors. If so, there may be a conflict of interests, and at the very least, the buyer will need to check the supplier's policies and practices on the protection of confidential data and intellectual property.

2.19 **Organisation culture** ('the way we do things around here') is a reflection of the shared values, beliefs, assumptions and norms of behaviour that develop in an organisation over time. It is explicitly stated in corporate mission and values statements, but is also visible in the attitudes expressed by managers and staff, in their behaviour, in the 'look' of the premises, the neatness of staff uniforms – and all sorts of other expressions. How does the supplier 'feel' about quality and customer service? Is it committed to innovation, creativity, responsibility, ethics and/or the environment? Are employees motivated and quality-conscious, or do they cut corners where possible? How effective is communication within the company? Such things will be an important indicator of the supplier's capability and commitment, and whether constructive working relationships will be possible with the buyer. The culture of the supplier may simply be incompatible with that of the buyer: their values, or attitudes to quality, or tolerance for risk, say, may simply be too different to allow for collaboration or the management of expectations.

2.20 The **identified costs of the proposed purchase** will obviously be a key factor in evaluation of a potential supplier – although price may not be directly relevant at the pre-qualification stage. What the buyer will be interested in, however, is:

- How the supplier's costs are structured and allocated, and therefore whether it will be able to offer competitive prices
- Whether the supplier may be willing and able to commit to collaborative cost reduction initiatives
- Whether discounts (eg for bulk purchase or early payment) or extended payment terms may be available
- The total acquisition and ownership costs of the proposed purchase: looking beyond the purchase price of the item, to the costs of after-sales service, warranties, maintenance contracts, spare parts, user training, consumables, waste-products disposal, end-of-life product disposal or recycling and so on.

Models for supplier appraisal

2.21 A helpful checklist of areas for supplier investigation is suggested by Ray Carter's '10 Cs of supplier evaluation'.

- Competency of all staff all of the time: this includes managers, sales staff, technical and production staff etc
- Capacity of supplier (must have sufficient, flexible production capacity; must have sufficient financial capability)

- Commitment to quality, evidenced by quality systems and perhaps by external accreditation such as ISO 9000
- Control of processes (again ISO 9000 may be relevant)
- Cash (must be financially sound)
- Cost (total acquisition cost, including extras, must be competitive)
- Consistency of output, delivery and service
- Culture (must be compatible with buyer organisation)
- Clean (ie environmentally sound)
- Compliance (or corporate social responsibility)

2.22 Another model, even easier to remember and popular with examiners, is the **FACE 2 FACE** checklist (originated by Dawn Dadds): Table 7.2.

Table 7.2 *The FACE 2 FACE model of supplier appraisal*

Fixed assets Physical resources to meet buyer needs	**F**inancial stability For continuity of supply
Ability to deliver the goods Production capacity and reliability of delivery, quality and service	**A**bility to work with the buyer Compatibility of culture, contacts, willingness to co-operate
Cost Competitive total acquisition costs, willingness to negotiate terms	**C**ommitment to quality Reliability of quality standards and systems, willingness to improve
Efficiency Use of resources, minimisation of waste	**E**nvironmental/ethical factors Policies and practices on CSR

Methods used to gather the information

2.23 Having looked at what information will be looked for, how does the buyer go about getting it? Common methods include: the use of appraisal questionnaires completed by suppliers; perusal of the supplier's financial statements and reports; checking the supplier's certifications, accreditations, quality awards, policy statements and so on; arranging to get references from existing customers; and checking product samples or portfolios of work.

2.24 There is no one ideal method of supplier appraisal, and a combination of methods may be used, according to the circumstances and the importance of the purchase. The method used will partly depend on the importance of the item being purchased: standardised or low-value purchases will not warrant rigorous, expensive methods such as site visits or third party assessments, for example.

2.25 Quite a lot of the information which is most easily gathered about suppliers is provided by suppliers themselves. Naturally, a buyer will need to recognise that such information is unlikely to be unbiased, and may be deliberately designed to show the supplier in the best possible light (eg in the case of sales and marketing communications) – if not positively misleading.

2.26 Various methods of appraising suppliers can also be seen as ways of 'verifying information provided by suppliers' – for example, as part of a tender or quotation – or verifying supplier capabilities. Some authorities separate coverage of methods of supplier appraisal (such as supplier questionnaires and site visits) from methods of verifying supplier capabilities (such as reference checking, financial assessment and capability audits) – but we can see no compelling reason for doing so. Many of the methodologies will be the same, whether the buyer is investigating a supplier proactively, in order to pre-qualify it, or in order to verify claims or promises in a quotation or tender bid.

3 Information for supplier appraisal

3.1 As we saw from Section 1 of this chapter, a number of basic information search methods can be used to appraise suppliers. These include:

- *Reputation*: seeking recommendations, reports and testimonials from industry analysts, trade associations, press write-ups, networking with other buyers and so on
- *Approvals and accreditations*: checking to see if the supplier appears on the approved or accredited registers of suppliers and stockists of major organisations or standards certification bodies (eg if it is accredited under ISO 9000 or 14000, or has won a quality award)

3.2 However, more proactive methods of appraising suppliers are outlined below.

Supplier questionnaires

3.3 Detailed questionnaires should be sent to the potential supplier for completion, posing a range of evaluation questions across the areas discussed in Section 2 above. Many firms use multi-page checklists similar to vendor rating forms. The answers are analysed by the buyer, and scored according to a predetermined marking scheme. The supplier can then be rated, for named products or processes, as 'fully approved', 'approved', 'conditionally approved' (requiring improvement) or 'unapproved'.

Site visit and capability survey

3.4 Where a potential supplier is accessible, the buyer may use a supplier audit or site visit: a visit to the supplier's premises by a cross-functional appraisal team (eg with experts on procurement, quality assurance and engineering, say). The team shares responsibility for the decision to approve or reject the supplier on the basis of their observations. A supplier visit can be used for the following purposes.

- To confirm information provided by the supplier in an appraisal questionnaire
- To observe and discuss, in greater detail, the supplier's premises, personnel, equipment, processes (particularly quality management) and outputs
- To enable the buyer to make personal contact with supplier-side account managers and other individuals whose co-operation will be relied on if delivery or other problems occur.

3.5 A *capability survey*, carried out as part of supplier audit, is designed to gather detailed information about the supplier's capabilities.

- *Technical or production capabilities*: its operating capacity, R & D capability, quality management systems, equipment and maintenance, workforce training and productivity and so on
- *Financial capabilities*: financial ratios indicating the company's efficiency, cashflow position, debt and profitability
- *Commercial capabilities*: customer account management, order handling procedures and systems, e-business systems, distribution channels, lead times for delivery and so on

- *Environmental capabilities*: environmental policy, accredited environmental management systems (eg ISO14000), carbon footprint assessment systems, pollution controls, recovery and recycling procedures, waste or end-of-life disposal methods, 'green' sourcing and so on.

References

3.6 We noted earlier that one source of information on suppliers is to ask the opinion of their current or previous customers. One approach to this is to ask potential suppliers for the contact details of selected customers ('references') and to contact those customers to ask about their experience with the supplier ('taking up' the references). Alternatively, the supplier may supply written references or testimonials from customers, which the buyer may follow up by phone (or with a more in-depth questionnaire) to get more details and a less 'prepared' view. You have probably come across similar procedures when applying for a job or renting accommodation.

3.7 In either case, you may feel that you are likely to be getting 'positive spin' rather than an unbiased picture, and it may be advisable rather to ask the supplier for its customer list, and permission to contact customers of *your* choice. Suppliers may resist this on quite reasonable grounds (eg to protect the privacy or confidentiality of its customers), but you might still be wary – and choose not to rely solely on any references the supplier provides.

3.8 The purpose of references is to gather a third party (theoretically, objective) view of the supplier's capabilities and performance, and what they are like to deal with. In taking up or following up references (by phone, questionnaire or – for major contracts – personal interview), you might ask a range of questions about areas of interest.

- How would the referee rate the supplier's quality, consistency or service (and how does the referee measure these things)?
- How would the referee rate the supplier's flexibility, responsiveness, innovation, communication?
- What does the referee regard as the supplier's strengths and weaknesses?
- Can the referee cite any critical incidents of excellent or poor quality or service?
- Where there have been quality or service issues, how serious were they, how frequently did they occur, and how co-operative was the supplier in resolving the problems?
- Would the referee use the supplier again, definitely or with some qualification?

Financial appraisal

3.9 As we saw earlier, a buyer will be interested in a number of aspects of a potential supplier's financial structure, performance and stability – especially for long-term contracts and supply relationships. Financial information about suppliers can be obtained from various sources.

- Their published financial statements and accounts: balance sheet, profit and loss account and cashflow statements
- Analysis of financial statements and results in the business or trade press
- Credit rating companies (such as Dun & Bradstreet).

3.10 The detail of financial analysis is beyond the scope of this syllabus.

Work sampling

3.11 One key way to appraise supplier quality, and/or to verify supplier quality claims, is to evaluate the products or services themselves. This may be done by:

- Requesting samples of the supplier's products, for evaluation
- Randomly sampling the outputs of the supplier's production process, as part of a site visit: that is, inspecting selected items as they come off the production line and/or after they have passed quality control inspection
- Sampling the supplier's products and service with a small trial order
- Sampling the supplier's services with a small test contract, or trial period.

Ability to manage specific requirements

3.12 So far, we have considered supplier appraisal in relatively general terms such as quality, service and capability. However, the buyer may have particular or unusual requirements, on which it will want to evaluate the supplier's capability, or verify the supplier's claims.

3.13 *High-volume order requirements* are a key example. How can the buyer evaluate or verify the supplier's capacity to supply high volumes on demand, without compromise on quality, and at a price that reflects the expected economies of scale?

- Estimated volumes and maximum potential volumes should be discussed with the potential supplier from the start.
- Suppliers should be asked to provide evidence of any claim to be able to support high-volume production. This may take the form of productivity records, reports of output volumes for previous similar projects, the opportunity to talk to previous or existing high-volume-purchasing customers, or the opportunity to view and audit production outputs at the supplier's factory.
- Test contracts or pilot projects may be used to verify the supplier's capacity in a controlled area.
- The supplier's infrastructure to support volume production (eg its supply chain management) should be examined.
- The contingency plans of the supplier for co-opting extra capacity if required (eg available quality-assured suppliers) should also be examined.

3.14 Other attributes or requirements that the buyer may want to ascertain, verify or test include the following.

- Responsiveness to urgent orders
- The ability to sustain just in time (demand-driven) supply
- The ability to offer late customisation or late finishing of products: holding stock of work in progress for end-consumer-driven customisation
- Contribution to innovation (eg through early supplier involvement): access to leading edge technologies, investment in research and development, knowledge-gathering and knowledge-sharing capabilities; and so on
- Readiness for e-sourcing and e-procurement arrangements.

3.15 In cases where the buyer foresees significant supply risk (eg if a supplier is not ISO 9000 accredited, or is an offshore supplier, or is being considered for outsourcing of a key organisational function), the appraisal will have to be wider and deeper.

4 Measuring supplier performance

4.1 There are various good reasons to put effort into evaluating supplier performance. According to Lysons & Farrington, supplier performance appraisal can:

- Help identify the highest-quality and best-performing suppliers: assisting decision-making regarding: (a) which suppliers should get specific orders (or be invited to tender for a contract); (b) when a supplier should be retained or removed from a preferred or approved list; and (c) which suppliers show potential for closer partnership relationships.
- Suggest how relationships with suppliers can (or need to be) enhanced to improve their performance (eg to evaluate the effectiveness of procurement's supplier selection and contract management processes)
- Help ensure that suppliers live up to what was promised in their contracts
- Provide suppliers with an incentive to maintain and/or continuously improve performance levels
- Significantly improve supplier performance, by identifying problems which can be tracked and fixed, or areas in which support and development is needed.

4.2 Remember that *supplier appraisal* (pre-contract, for the purposes of supplier selection) is a somewhat different process from *supplier performance appraisal* (post-contract, for the purposes of management control). The former assesses a potential supplier's capability to fulfil the buyer's requirements; the latter assesses a current supplier's performance in fulfilling them. In order to distinguish the two more clearly, the post-contract process is sometimes referred to as **vendor rating**: a vendor being a person or organisation that currently sells you something, and rating being a way of evaluating or 'scoring' performance.

4.3 Vendor rating is the measurement of supplier performance using agreed criteria, usually including:

- *Price*: eg measured by value for money, market price or under, lowest or competitive pricing, good cost management and reasonable profit margins
- *Quality*: eg measured by key performance indicators (KPIs) such as the number or proportion of defects, quality assurance procedures
- *Delivery*: eg measured by KPIs such as the proportion of on-time in-full (OTIF) deliveries, or increases or decreases in lead times for delivery

4.4 Other measurable factors might include: after-sales service, efficiency and accuracy of contract management and administration, willingness to commit to continuous improvement, quality of contacts and communication, contribution to innovation, flexibility and responsiveness to urgent or unusual requests – and so on.

4.5 There are two basic approaches to vendor rating. One common approach is based on the use of a *supplier performance evaluation form*: a checklist of key performance factors, against which purchasers assess the supplier's performance as good, satisfactory or unsatisfactory: Figure 7.1. A *weighting* is applied to each factor, so that the supplier's performance in key performance areas, and overall, can be summarised as good, satisfactory or unsatisfactory. This is comparatively easy to implement, once meaningful checklists have been developed, but it is fairly broad and subjective.

Figure 7.1 *Extract from a supplier evaluation form (adapted from Dobler & Burt)*

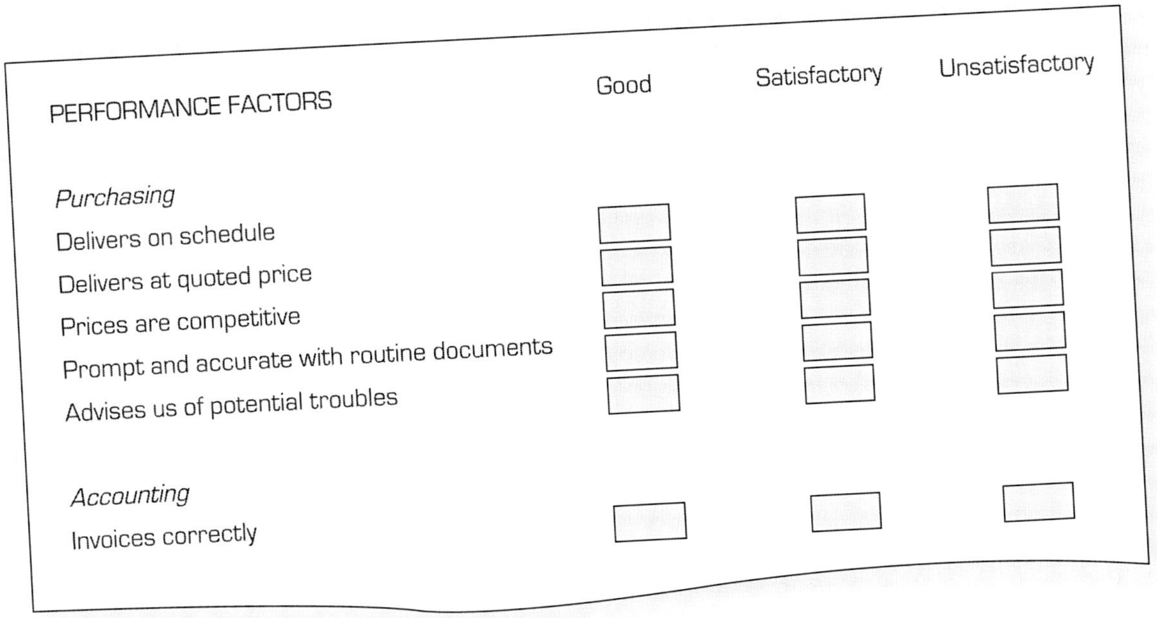

```
PERFORMANCE FACTORS              Good    Satisfactory   Unsatisfactory

Purchasing
Delivers on schedule              ☐         ☐              ☐
Delivers at quoted price          ☐         ☐              ☐
Prices are competitive            ☐         ☐              ☐
Prompt and accurate with routine documents  ☐   ☐         ☐
Advises us of potential troubles  ☐         ☐              ☐

Accounting
Invoices correctly                ☐         ☐              ☐
```

4.6 Another approach is the *factor rating method*. The idea is to pick out key factors such as price, quality and delivery, and to determine a numerical method of measurement for each. (For example, the measure of quality performance might be '100% minus percentage of rejects in total deliveries'. A supplier whose deliveries contained 3% rejects would score 97% or 0.97 on this measure.) Each of the major factors is given a weighting, according to its importance within overall performance, and this is applied to the score given to the supplier on each factor, to end up with an overall score or rating. We showed an example of this in Chapter 4 (repeated below for convenience).

Performance factor	Weighting	Supplier's score	Supplier rating
Price	0.4	0.94	0.376
Quality	0.4	0.97	0.388
Delivery	0.2	0.82	0.164
Overall evaluation	1.0		0.928

4.7 The supplier in our example has achieved a rating of 0.928 out of a possible 1. This score can be compared with that achieved by other suppliers, and gives a good measure of exactly where each stands in the order of preference. It may also be used year on year, to provide a measure of whether a supplier's performance is improving or declining.

4.8 Of course, neither approach diagnoses the causes of any performance shortfalls identified, nor what needs to be done to address them. A vendor rating should therefore be seen within the whole process of performance management.

Chapter summary

- Sourcing means identifying potential suppliers capable of fulfilling an identified need. There are numerous sources of information that can help, such as the buyer's own database, communications from suppliers etc.
- Once potential suppliers have been identified it may be appropriate to pre-qualify them. This is to ensure that they are capable of performing any contract that may eventually be awarded.
- Criteria for supplier evaluation include financial status, capacity, technical capability, systems and procedures, conformance to legislation, and the supplier's supply chain, customer base and culture.
- Models for supplier appraisal include Carter's 10 Cs, and FACE 2 FACE.
- Methods of gathering information for supplier appraisal include supplier questionnaires, site visits and capability surveys, trade references, analysis of published financial information and work sampling.
- A supplier's published financial statements will provide important information about profitability, liquidity, gearing, working capital and financial stability.
- Information for supplier appraisal can come from sources such as questionnaires, site visits and references.
- After contract award, it is important to monitor supplier performance. Vendor rating is a formal method of doing so.

Self-test questions

Numbers in brackets refer to paragraphs where you can check your answers.

1. List sources of information to identify potential suppliers. (1.3)

2. What information about existing suppliers might be included in a buyer's database? (1.4 and Table 7.1)

3. What is the purpose of supplier appraisal? (2.1)

4. What criteria might be used in the pre-qualification of suppliers? (2.5)

5. List the factors identified by the FACE 2 FACE model. (2.22 and Table 7.2)

6. What are the purposes of a supplier site visit? (3.4)

7. How can a buyer assess a supplier's potential to supply high-volume order requirements? (3.13)

8. What factors will typically be assessed in a vendor rating exercise? (4.3)

CHAPTER 8
Formation of Agreements

Assessment criteria and indicative content

2.4 Explain approaches to the formation of agreements with external organisations

- Dealing with queries and clarifications
- Ensuring transparency and fairness with suppliers
- Mistakes and second bids in tenders
- The use of reverse auctions/e-auctions
- Forming agreements with customers and suppliers
- Transition and mobilisation arrangements

Section headings

1. Formation of contracts
2. The contracting process
3. Transparency and fairness

Introduction

The formation of agreements between organisations is a fundamental part of business. The pre-agreement negotiation, the forming of the contract and the management of the contract are crucial business areas.

This chapter looks at the fundamentals required for forming a contract.

Unless otherwise noted, the law stated in this chapter is that of England and Wales, as exemplar.

1 Formation of contracts

Contract basics

1.1 A contract is an agreement reached between two or more parties which is legally enforceable when executed in accordance with specific requirements. The contract will be entered into voluntarily by two parties or more with the intention of creating a legal obligation. In a business setting it would be expected that the contract would be in writing, though in principle this may not be essential (depending on the country in which supplier and buyer form the agreement).

1.2 Contracts are obviously a key part of every business and it is fundamental that all parties to a contract understand the terms and conditions included and the rights and responsibilities of the parties.

1.3 Every contract must have the following basic elements.

- Offer (for example, a buyer offers to purchase 100 widgets at $2 per unit)
- Acceptance (for example, a supplier agrees to supply the widgets at that price)

- Consideration (something valuable from each party: in this case, $200 from the buyer, 100 widgets from the supplier)
- The intention to create legal relations (in other words, each party accepts that their obligations can be enforced if necessary by the relevant courts of law)

Terms of the contract

1.4 Contracts can be in writing, made orally, or created through the acts of the parties. For clarity, most commercial contracts are in writing to maintain a proper record of the agreement. Oral contracts create a greater potential for disputes on the terms agreed. The parties may have problems evidencing their position.

1.5 Contracts can be formed through a course of trading between the parties. As with oral contracts the terms and conditions may not be clear in such a case. Common terms and conditions are likely to be incorporated in these contracts but if they are not written down problems may occur.

1.6 It is common for contracts to be on a company's 'Standard Terms and Conditions'. Issues can arise when both parties purport to contract on their own standard terms and conditions *(a situation known as the battle of the forms)*.

1.7 There are different approaches for those parties who wish to contract on their own terms and conditions including incorporating the terms into as many pre-contractual documents as possible and ensuring that the terms appear on the last document between the parties before the delivery of the goods or service.

Essential terms

1.8 Below we look at the main terms that would be expected to appear in any contract.

1.9 **Parties**: The names and adresses (including registered addresses) of all the contracting parties.

1.10 **Definitions and interpretations**: If there are any defined terms in the contract this section should provide specific and clear definitions.

1.11 **Payment provisions**: The exact price to be paid for the goods or services provided and the date or dates for payment. It may be relevant to provide for adjustments to the price due to occurrence of certain events, such as rising commodity prices, inflation or exchange rate movements. This section should also note any agreed rate of interest payable on overdue amounts and the consequences of failure to pay.

1.12 **A specific description of the goods or services** that will be provided under the contract including the level of service if the contract is for services. This section should also include who is responsible for supporting and maintaining any products throughout the term of the contract.

1.13 **Term of contract**: the length of the contract should be stated and it should also be noted whether there are any options to continue the contract. For example, 'This agreement will continue for another year unless notified (to the other party) by January 31 each year'.

1.14 **Timescale**: the specific timescale for the project should be noted (if applicable) including any deadlines that have to be met. This section should include any pre-agreed payments (liquidated damages) payable by the supplier if deadlines are not met.

1.15 **Limitation of liability**: this section places a cap on the liability of either party to the contract. For example, 'Neither party shall have any liability to the other party for a claim of loss of profits'. In an ideal world both parties would be seeking to have no liability to the other side. However in a commercial context this is unlikely and so both parties should try to limit their liability during the negotiation stage.

1.16 **Termination provisions**: the circumstances under which the parties can terminate the contract should be stated clearly. The procedure for giving notice to the other party should be stated. For example, 'This agreement can be terminated by either party giving at least three months written notice'.

1.17 **Change of control**: during the course of a contract one party may change the structure of their company. In these circumstances the other party may wish to terminate the contract. For example, this might happen if the first party transfers a controlling interest to a competitor of the other party. The procedure for dealing with this situation should be in the contract.

1.18 **Dispute resolution**: the procedure to be followed if the parties have a dispute should be included (for example, an option for arbitration or mediation where the issue cannot be resolved through internal escalation).

1.19 **Confidentiality**: contracts often deal with commercially sensitive information and the parties are likely to want to keep this information confidential. There should be confidentiality clauses drafted in the contract which identify the information being protected and the circumstances in which it can be used or discussed.

1.20 **Intellectual property rights**: many commercial contracts include a clause stating who will own the intellectual property right to any products provided under the contracts. This clause should specifically state who owns such rights. Particular attention should be given to ownership of intellectual property rights in relation to products created specifically for or in connection with the contract.

1.21 **Warranties**: it is usual for the party providing goods and services under the contract to provide certain warranties in relation to the delivery of the goods or services. Warranties give the other party a contractual right to sue for damages if there is a breach of warranty.

1.22 **Indemnity**: indemnity clauses are an express obligation to compensate the indemnified party by making a money payment for some defined loss or damage. They provide for an immediate right to compensation, without the need for a lengthy dispute as to the circumstances giving rise to the specified loss or damage.

1.23 *Force majeure*: this clause should cover situations where performance of the contract is impossible through no fault of either party (for example, if there is a natural disaster or civil unrest).

1.24 **Applicable law**: there should be a clause indicating which country's law governs the contract.

Implied terms

1.25 Certain terms may be implied into contracts by law, or by usage or custom. For example, it is normally implied that the supplier of goods or services must provide goods of satisfactory quality which are fit for the buyer's purpose, even if this is not specifically stated in the contract.

Contract management

1.26 Once the contract has been concluded it is important to monitor its performance. Often there are governance mechanisms set out in the contract which govern the relationship between the parties, and provide forums to monitor performance and deal with change. Internally, each party should check that the other is fulfilling its obligations and that timescales and payment plans in the contract are being adhered to.

2 The contracting process

Contract administration

2.1 Contract administration is concerned with the operational relationship between the buyer and the supplier, the implementation of procedures defining the working methods and practices between them, and the smooth operation of routine administrative and clerical functions.

2.2 The importance of contract administration (both buyers' and suppliers' procedures) to the success of the contract, and to the relationship between them, should not be underestimated. Clear administrative procedures ensure that all parties to the contract understand who does what, when, and how.

2.3 Contract administration will require appropriate resourcing. It may be that the responsibility falls on a nominated individual. If not, and the responsibility is shared across a contract management team, it is important that all members of the team deal promptly with contract administration tasks, particularly during the early stages of implementing the new contract arrangements.

2.4 The procedures that usually make up contract administration are as follows.

- Contract maintenance and change control
- Charges and cost monitoring
- Ordering procedures
- Payment procedures
- Budget procedures
- Resource management and planning
- Management reporting
- Escalation
- Dispute resolution

2.5 These procedures should be designed to reflect the specific circumstances of the contract and the organisation. Bear in mind that additional administrative procedures may also be needed.

2.6 Contractual relationships evolve and must respond to changes in the business environment. It follows that the contract document itself must be capable of development through formal change control procedures and by mutual consent, in response to changing requirements. It is preferable to update documentation as changes occur rather than relying on informal arrangements.

2.7 Keeping the contract documentation up to date is an important activity, but it should not be a burden. The effort required may be reduced by ensuring that the contract is sufficiently flexible to enable changes to the requirement and pricing mechanism within agreed parameters without needing to change the contract documentation.

2.8   Procedures should be established to keep the contract documentation up to date and to ensure that all documents relating to the contract are consistent, and that all parties have a common view. For a large or complex contract, or a situation where a number of service level agreements (SLAs) are covered, a formal document management procedure is critically important. Some form of change control procedure is needed for all contracts.

2.9   Applying document management principles involves:
- identifying all relevant documentation (including contract clauses and schedules, SLAs, procedures manuals etc)
- change control procedures, and ensuring no changes are made without appropriate authorisation
- recording the status of documents (current or historic, draft or final)
- ensuring consistency across documents.

2.10 It is particularly important that additional demands on the supplier should be carefully controlled. In many cases orders for products or services may only be submitted through the contract manager. In other cases, especially where budgets are devolved, business managers may have authority to submit orders within specified budgetary and technical constraints. Formal authorisation procedures will be required to ensure that only those new requirements that can be justified in business terms are added to the contract.

2.11 Changes to the requirement, procedures or contracts may impact on supplier performance and costs. The specification and management of change control is an important area of contract administration. Change control procedures should be included in the contract. The respective roles and responsibilities of both parties in the change control process must be clearly identified, along with the procedures for raising, evaluating, costing and approving change requests.

2.12 A single change control procedure should apply to all changes, although there may be certain delegated or shortened procedures available in defined circumstances, such as delegated budget tolerance levels within which a contract manager would not have to seek senior management approval. However, flexibility should be built into this procedure to deal with issues such as emergencies.

2.13 Requirements for performance reports and management information should have been defined before and during contract negotiations, and confirmed during the transition period of the contract. It is likely that information requirements will change during the lifetime of the contract, which should be flexible enough to allow for this. Where possible, use should be made of the supplier's own management information and performance measurement systems.

2.14 Information may be required about all performance measures or only about exceptions – that is, instances when performance differs from what was expected. 'Exception reporting' minimises the time the buyer needs to assess performance and ensures attention is focused on areas that need it most.

Improving performance

2.15 Incentives to improve are normally built into the contract terms. The aim of incentives is to motivate the supplier to improve by offering increased profit, or some other desirable benefit, as a reward for improved performance or added value. It is important that incentives are balanced. They should not emphasise one aspect of performance at the expense of other, perhaps less visible, aspects. The aim is value for money at all levels, rather than simple cost savings. Here are some examples of incentives.

- Guaranteed or fixed levels of capacity, allowing the planning of investments and improvements by the provider
- Revenue sharing, gain sharing, or tariff reduction
- Opportunity for innovation: the contract gives the provider the chance to implement or devise new solutions that will improve their standing
- Key performance indicators (KPIs) for recognition and reward

2.16 Improvements could be expressed in terms of developments such as the following.

- Improved customer satisfaction, as measured, for example, by independent surveys
- More efficient ways of providing the specified requirement
- Useful additions to the specification
- Eliminating aspects of the requirement that are no longer required
- Use of new technologies that would reduce costs but improve quality of the product or service
- Changes in procedures or working practices

Problems, queries and clarifications

2.17 However good the relationship between buyer and supplier, problems may arise. So procedures for handling these should be agreed; clear reporting and escalation procedures help keep the heat out of the relationship. The objective is a relationship in which purchaser and supplier co-operate to ensure that problems are recognised and then resolved quickly and effectively.

2.18 The contract must define the procedures for undertaking corrective action if, for example, target performance levels are not being achieved. The purchaser response to non-performance should be commensurate with the severity of the failure. For certain types of failure, the contract may specify the application of 'liquidated damages'; procedures are required to calculate these and to enforce them. Problems can arise in a number of areas and for a wide range of reasons: clashes of personality; slow or incorrect submission of invoices; slow payment of invoices; problems with contract administration procedures.

2.19 If a dispute cannot be resolved at the level where it arises, it will be necessary to involve a more senior manager. Escalation procedures should allow for successive levels of response depending on the nature of the problem and the outcome of action taken at lower levels. The levels for escalation should match those of the interfaces established between the buyer and the supplier to resolve the problem at the lowest practicable level. For more serious problems, the contract should specify the circumstances under which the organisation would have the right to terminate the contract. The contract manager must consult senior management and procurement or contractual advisors as soon as this possibility arises.

2.20 Normally, most problems should be resolved before they become major issues; contract managers on both sides should meet regularly to raise any issues promptly as they occur. In extreme cases, where agreement cannot be reached, the purchaser and supplier should seek the assistance of mediators before resorting to legal action. The contract should specify the procedures for invoking a formal dispute resolution process.

2.21 The contract managers from both buyer and supplier organisations should meet on a regular basis to review performance and delivery of the contract outputs. There may well be regular issues to discuss (eg customer feedback, complaints log) that will be standing items on the meeting agenda. Other agenda items will probably relate to particular queries or clarifications during the period under review. All meetings should be minuted, with clear action points allocated to named individuals from both the supplier and buyer organisations. The action points should have dates for completion, and these should then be reviewed, and any problems highlighted at the next review meeting.

Transition and mobilisation arrangements

2.22   Towards the end of the contract period, the contract manager from the buyer's organisation should be involved with a full review conducted by the business of the contracted out area. If a decision is taken by the business that the need still remains, then the contract manager is well placed, through their practical knowledge of the current operational requirements, to advise on any updating or modification to the specification of requirement. In most circumstances it is inadvisable merely to re-use the same specification of requirement for a further contract period, with either the existing or the new supplier.

2.23   If a new supplier is to be used it may well be necessary for the new supplier to contact the old supplier to obtain information. It should be specified in the contract that the existing supplier is required to co-operate with such transition arrangements.

2.24   Once the new supplier has all the information required the buyer can 'mobilise' the new contract. In other words, the buyer will commence regular dealings with the new supplier, most likely on very similar contractual terms to those that went before.

2.25   The contract managers from both the buyer's and supplier's organisations need to set the stage early for working together in managing the performance of the contract. The relationship will be underpinned by the contract and service level agreement, but much will depend on the ability of the contract managers to work as a team towards the delivery of the contractually agreed outputs.

3   Transparency and fairness

3.1   Sharing plans and information about potential future objectives can help ensure the parties develop the relationship in line with changes in business need. This should be a two-way process. An understanding of where the supplier sees its business going is as important as the buyer's expectations if divergent positions are not to evolve unexpectedly.

3.2   Sharing information with suppliers may raise concerns about how information will be used. There may, for example, be a concern that information about the buyer's organisation plans, finances and resources will be exploited by a supplier for its own commercial advantage. Willingness to share information openly depends largely on the element of trust.

3.3   Information about how the supplier views the buyer should also be sought. Here again, a candid approach should be encouraged – although there is a need to avoid being defensive about criticism. The focus should be on providing and seeking information with a view to improving the relationship over time rather than apportioning blame.

3.4   Everyone involved in the relationship should be ready to learn from the mistakes and experience of others. The emphasis in providing and accepting feedback on performance should be on using such information as a basis for improvement rather than penalty.

3.5 Transparency and fairness are a two-way process. Buyers must ensure transparency and fairness in the way they deal with suppliers. Equally, buyers should expect a high level of transparency and fairness from suppliers.

3.6 In terms of the buyer's own behaviour, it is important to be honest with suppliers about the exact requirement. It is not fair or ethical to inflate the likely requirement in order to get a better price (and subsequently letting the supplier down). Equally it is wrong to encourage supplier's to quote when there is no real intention of dealing with them (as buyers have been known to do, with a view to getting better terms from another supplier).

3.7 By the same token, the buyer will look for transparency from the supplier. Suppliers will often present prices as a total figure without a breakdown of the various elements of which they are comprised. In the case of important, strategic procurements the buyer may ask for more detail about the supplier's costs. His aim would be to check whether the supplier's prices are reasonable.

3.8 For procurement professionals, the task is to analyse the pricing to understand the various elements that make up the suppliers costs and margins. This places the purchaser in a stronger position in the negotiation process.

3.9 In the current economic climate there is a tendency for suppliers to provide less transparency in the make-up of their costs. Pressures are forcing suppliers to maximise the margin in every element of their cost structure and bundling all the cost components together enables them to conceal the margins they have built in to their total price more effectively.

3.10 The cost of different materials and components often varies widely between suppliers even though the final price of an item may be similar. This means that if procurement can identify the supplier's costs and margins by 'unbundling' the cost components they will be able to negotiate prices for the constituent parts of an item as well as the total cost.

3.11 This approach to transparency also ensures that the supplier's profit margins more accurately reflect market conditions, creating the additional benefit that the relationship with the buyer will be more sustainable in the longer term as both parties are likely to be happier if the deal makes economic sense from their own perspective.

Reverse auctions/e-auctions

3.12 A reverse auction is an electronic auction where suppliers bid online against each other for contracts against a published specification.

3.13 In a normal auction, a company or an individual will offer an item for sale and bidders will offer what they think the item is worth, with the price increasing as the bids mount. In an online auction, such as eBay, the auction will have a time limit with the winner of the auction having the highest bid when the time expires.

3.14 In reverse auctions, a buyer will offer a contract on which a number of suppliers will bid, based on the terms and conditions of the contract. The company that has the lowest bid when the reverse auction expires is the winner of the contract.

3.15 Often other factors (such as existing business relationships, reputation of suppliers, delivery time and quality) will influence the buyer. In theory the reverse auction is decided on price, but in practice other factors influence the buyer's decision.

3.16 In recent years reverse auctions have grown in business use by both the private and the public sector for the procurement of goods and services. The growth has been driven by competitive forces in the procurement market together with the development of software packages that enable suppliers to compete with each other from remote locations.

3.17 Reverse auctions bring a number of benefits to the buyer.
- Elimination of paper and streamlined processes
- Short negotiation cycle
- Value for money procurement
- Increased transparency of the contract award process

3.18 By conducting contract negotiations online, the process is much quicker than the normal negotiation process. Reverse auctions create an environment where suppliers bid against each other for a contract. This environment encourages competition with the result that goods and services are offered at their current market value. Reduced paperwork, short procurement cycle and increased transparency of competing bids are clear benefits to suppliers.

3.19 The suitability for products to be offered in a reverse auction will depend on a number of factors.
- Specification of the product or service. A reverse auction may be suitable for a product or service that is reasonably straightforward. A product that has a specification requiring detailed explanations or customisation would be beyond the scope of a reverse auction. Products that are suitable are commodities or near commodities, generic products such as certain prescription drugs or office stationery etc.
- Lead time. If a company requires a fast response then reverse auctions may not be suitable. A supplier (who may need pre-qualification) requires time to put together their best bid and the lowest price they are prepared to go to.
- Quantity required. The volume of items or the value of the overall contract offered must be large enough to make hosting the reverse auction worthwhile from both the purchaser's and the supplier's standpoint.
- Number of vendors. For a reverse auction to be successful a customer must offer an item or service where a minimum of three suitable suppliers are bidding on the auction. If there are not enough suitable suppliers, the item or service would be better managed through direct negotiation.

Mistakes in tenders

3.20 The **tender document** provides all information and instructions relative to the tender's administrative, technical and financial requirements, as well as indicating the selection and award criteria that will be applied. The tender may be by submission of documents or by a reverse auction.

- Always provide all of the information requested in the tender application.
- It is important that the calculations of tender prices are correct.
- Often, tenderers misinterpret the scope of the work. If you are unsure of anything in the tender, ask.

- Always sign your bid document. Unsigned documents will be disqualified.
- Make sure that you deliver the tender in the prescribed manner by the prescribed time and get a receipt.
- If *samples* are requested, sufficient amounts must be supplied to enable the item to be evaluated under the appropriate technical or clinical conditions.

3.21 There are a number of simple rules for avoiding mistakes in tenders.

- Always read through the bid documents carefully.
- Complete the document in full.
- Do a proper cost analysis when calculating bid prices. Bids calculated too high or too low are considered unresponsive.
- Inquire about the bid and obtain all the relevant information before completing the tender document.
- Feel free to ask why you were unsuccessful so that you may learn from mistakes made (post-tender debrief).
- Make sure that you are able to meet all the requirements within the specified time and are able to honour your offer in the event that your bid is successful.
- Do not make any misrepresentations or false statements in your bid documentation. It is a legal document and therefore enforceable by law.

3.22 Mistakes are avoidable but if made can cause major issues. When a mistake is made, contact the procurement officer with responsibility for the contract immediately and detail the mistake. Public sector tenders, in particular, are governed by a stringent set of rules and regulations which address many issues. If the response of the procurement officer does not address the situation satisfactorily there are set procedures to escalate your concern.

3.23 Tender advertisements may not always specify the existence of an active complaints procedure. However in all cases there *will* actually be a complaints procedure. If it is not described in the tender documents themselves (which should certainly be the case), information on it will be accessible via the procurement officer for the contract in question.

Second bids

3.24 Evaluation of tenders is an area increasingly subject to challenges in the courts from bidders who are unhappy with the way in which public bodies have dealt with their bids. Bidders can potentially claim not only their wasted tender costs but also potential loss of profit for the contract.

3.25 As recent cases have indicated, it is not even necessary for unsuccessful bidders to prove that they would have been successful but for the evaluation errors. All they have to show is that they have been denied a fair attempt at the tender. The governance of the receipt, opening and contract award are designed to ensure the process is fair, equitable and robust.

3.26 As a result of this increased risk to the buyer, it is vital that a clear audit trail of the entire decision-making process throughout the evaluation process is maintained together with copies of all tenders submitted.

3.27 Points to be considered by the buyer:
- It is prudent to take legal advice if rejecting the bid

- Written records of evaluation must be kept
- Tenderers should be debriefed.

3.28 In certain cases errors and misunderstandings can occur. For example, the specification may be vague or open to interpretation in different ways. There is a process for raising questions related to tenders that ensures a fair and equitable response.

3.29 If the tenderer makes a complaint that is upheld, the tenderer will be given the opportunity to put forward a second bid if they wish. If that is not practical then the entire tender process may be required to recommence from the beginning. If the complaints procedure fails to resolve the situation the matter can be taken to arbitration or in certain cases to a court of law.

3.30 To re-run the tender again is an expensive and time-consuming operation for all parties involved. However, to ensure fairness and transparency in tender procurement it may be the only viable route.

Chapter summary

- Business agreements usually take the form of written contracts. For a contract to be valid, there must be offer, acceptance, consideration, and intention to form legal relations.
- The terms of a contract are mostly express (ie actually written out in the contract document), but a contract may also include implied terms.
- Contract administration is necessary to ensure a smooth working relationship between buyer and supplier.
- Transparency and fairness are a two-way process between buyer and supplier.
- Buyers must be fair to suppliers, and must avoid unethical practices (such as deliberately exaggerating the estimate of supply requirements).
- Equally, suppliers should be encouraged to display transparency and fairness, especially in the matter of their cost analysis.

Self-test questions

Numbers in brackets refer to paragraphs where you can check your answers.

1. What are the essential basic elements of a valid contract? (1.3)
2. List typical terms that might appear in a supply contract. (1.8–1.24)
3. List procedures that are typically involved in contract administration. (2.4)
4. Give examples of contractual incentives that might be offered to suppliers. (2.15)
5. Give examples of how buyers sometimes fail in their duty of fairness to suppliers. (3.6)
6. Explain how an online reverse auction works. (3.14)

CHAPTER 9

Electronic P2P Systems

Assessment criteria and indicative content

3.1 Explain the impact of electronic procure to pay (P2P) systems on procurement operations

- The stages of the sourcing process from identification of needs to the award of agreements
- Creating approvals and their timescales
- Defining procure to pay (P2P) systems
- Automating requisitions, purchase orders and invoices
- Integration of systems between organisations

Section headings

1. The procurement cycle
2. Identify and define requirements
3. Identify and select potential suppliers
4. Monitor, review and maintain performance
5. Procure-to-pay systems (P2P)
6. Integration of systems between organisations

Introduction

Procurement procedures and policies will naturally vary widely from one organisation to another – and even within organisations, according to different types of purchases. However, there are certain stages which a typical procurement transaction will involve, and this is known as the 'procurement cycle'.

In this chapter, we will look at the various stages of the procurement cycle, and at what happens during each stage. Our descriptions accord with general best practice – but of course we cannot incorporate all of the variations that will be experienced in your professional work, or in exam case studies. You will need to follow the policies and procedures of your own organisation in your day-to-day work.

The chapter also examines the impact of technology, in particular the use of 'procure-to-pay' (P2P) systems and their growth. It must be remembered that all the aspects of the procurement cycle and the accompanying best practice continue to apply.

P2P involves integration with other organisations both in terms of business relationships and technology. This chapter starts to examine the link between technology and business relationships. This theme will be developed further throughout the CIPS qualification.

There is a small amount of unavoidable repetition in this chapter. This is because Assessment Criterion 3.1 refers to the whole of the P2P cycle, whereas some aspects of the cycle were referred to in earlier Assessment Criteria, and hence discussed in earlier chapters.

1 The procurement cycle

1.1 The procurement cycle comprises all of the procurement activities that take place from the initial identification of need to the final satisfaction of that need.

1.2 The main stages of the procurement cycle are shown in Figure 9.1.

Figure 9.1 *The basic procurement cycle*

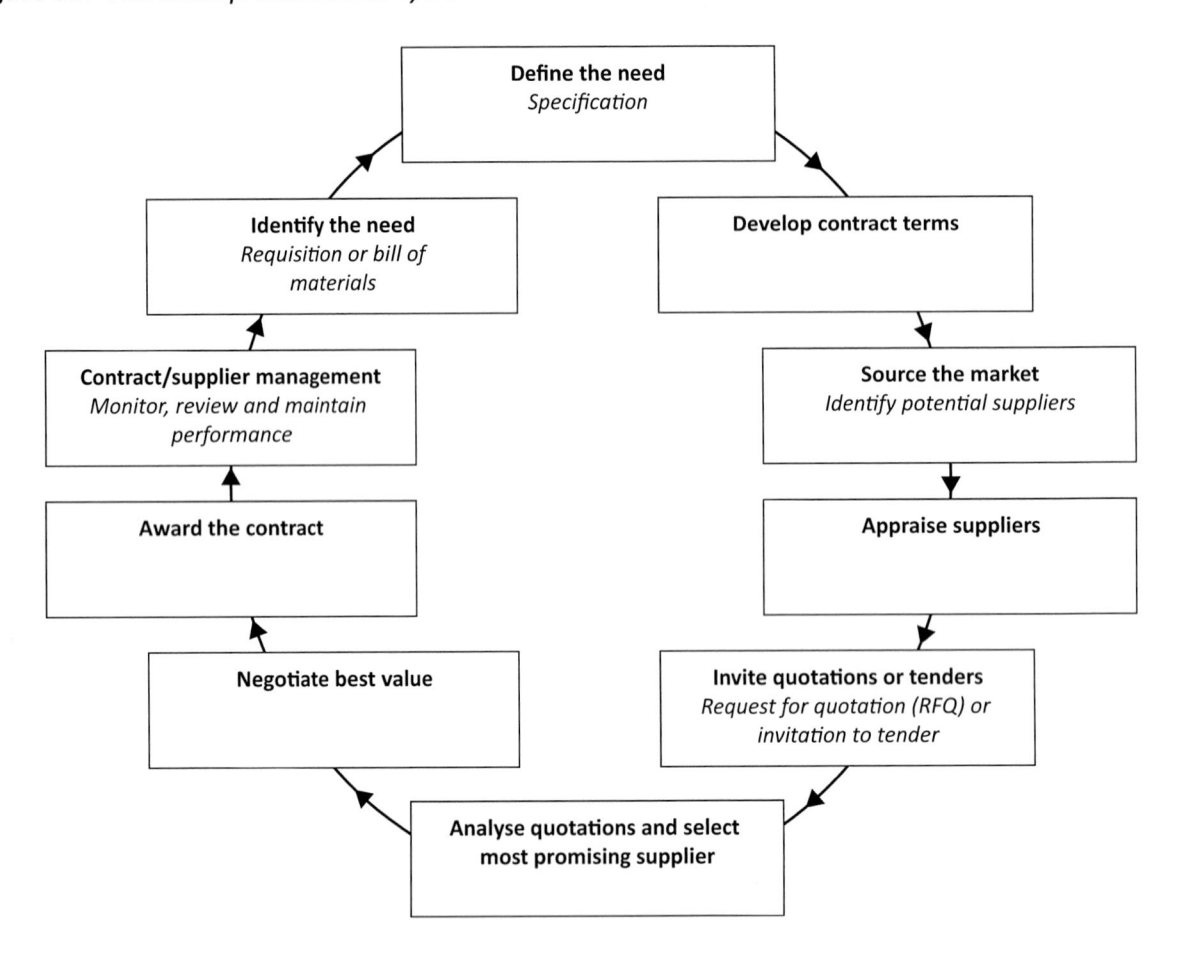

```
                    Define the need
                    Specification
                    ↑        ↓
        Identify the need         Develop contract terms
        Requisition or bill of              ↓
             materials
             ↑                        Source the market
                                      Identify potential suppliers
   Contract/supplier management              ↓
   Monitor, review and maintain
         performance                    Appraise suppliers
             ↑                              ↓
      Award the contract            Invite quotations or tenders
             ↑                      Request for quotation (RFQ) or
                                         invitation to tender
      Negotiate best value                  ↓
             ↖                        ↙
              Analyse quotations and select
                most promising supplier
```

1.3 Before we go on to explain the stages in detail, it is worth making a few general points.

1.4 Although you might think of this as a process, starting with the 'identify the need' stage and progressing to 'performance' (satisfaction of the need), it is – as the name implies – an ongoing cycle, because further needs will constantly emerge.

1.5 Not every purchase will follow every stage of the cycle. If a purchase is a **straight re-buy** of items already sourced from a supplier, for example, it will not be necessary to establish a specification, survey and source the market, invite quotations and select a supplier: the buyer may already have a preferred supplier (and perhaps a standing purchase agreement or 'call-off contract' with them). If it is a **modified re-buy**, in that some of the requirement has changed, it may be necessary to re-specify the need or re-negotiate the contract, but the same supplier may be used (or *vice versa*: the specification may stay the same, but a new supplier will be sought). **New buys** are more likely to conform to the full cycle.

1.6 The procurement cycle can be divided into two main stages.

- *Sourcing* is the part of the process concerned with 'how and where services or products are obtained' (CIPS): ie requirements definition, tendering, supplier selection and contract award.
- *Purchasing* is the part of the process concerned with the transactional aspects of purchase: requisitioning, authorising, ordering, receipting and payment.

Some key forms and documents in the procurement cycle

1.7 What are the key forms and documents used in the procurement cycle? We will be explaining each of these in the sections that follow, but to give you an overview we list them below.

- Purchase requisition or bill of materials (notification by users of a need for purchase)
- Specification and/or service level agreement
- Supplier appraisal questionnaire (for evaluation of potential supplier suitability)
- Request for quotation (RFQ) or invitation to tender (ITT)
- Supplier quotation, bid or tender documents
- Purchase order (or contract)
- Acknowledgement of order (from the supplier)
- Advice note (from the supplier, notifying delivery of the order)
- Goods received note (confirming receipt of the order)
- Quality inspection forms
- Invoice or statement (request for payment)
- Vendor rating forms (for appraising supplier performance).

1.8 We will now look at the key stages in the procurement cycle in detail.

2 Identify and define requirements

Identify the need: purchase requisition

2.1 Before any procurement transaction can begin, someone must notice that something is needed which is not currently available, and this need must be notified to the procurement department.

2.2 The need may be identified by a user department: for example, a designer may recognise the need for new software. Or the driver for purchase may come from a stores department: a check of inventory levels may reveal the need to replenish stocks of materials or components.

2.3 In either case, the normal procedure would be for the department concerned to raise a purchase requisition. This form describes the item needed and instigates action by the procurement department. Typically, the originator of the requisition would keep a copy of the form, while the other copy is forwarded as appropriate.

- If the originator is the stores department, the copy is forwarded to the procurement department.
- If the originator is a user department, the copy is forwarded to stores. Stores will meet the need if the item is in stock, and if not will pass the requisition on to procurement.

2.4 A purchase requisition form (whether printed or electronic) will typically include the following details.

- A description of the product or service required: identified by brand name or model number (if known), or accompanied by the specification (if already available)
- The quantity required
- The delivery or provision date

- The internal department code, or budgetary code, to which the expenditure is to be charged
- The name and signature of the originator of the requisition, and its date. This may act as an official authorisation of the need, giving procurement authority to act upon it, so the signature should be that of an individual with appropriate authority.

2.5 If the organisation operates a materials requirements planning (MRP) system, the identification of the need may instead be signalled by a **bill of materials (BOM)**. Briefly, the approach is to forecast the manufacturing schedule for finished products, and to translate this into details of the materials and parts needed for production: the bill of materials. This can then be compared with stock files, where relevant, to establish which materials and parts will have to be purchased.

2.6 Requisition and bill of materials forms will contain details of the required item(s) in a standardised form. However, procurement will not simply act on this description without enquiry. It may be appropriate to refer the requisition back to the originator: for clarification, or to challenge over-specification or unnecessary variation, or to suggest alternatives that will offer better quality or lower price than the item requisitioned.

Establish the specification

2.7 The process so far relates to the identification and description of the need *within* the buying organisation. The next step will be to establish and/or to communicate a detailed description of the requirement to potential suppliers. Detailed descriptions may already exist (if the purchase is a re-buy), but for new products or services, they may have to be drawn up, in the form of:

- Specifications (of various types)
- Service level agreements (added to the specification of services)
- Contract terms which set out the obligations of buyer and seller in relation to the fulfilment of the specification.

3 Identify and select potential suppliers

3.1 Where the item required is a standard or routine one, these stages of the sourcing cycle may be by-passed: preferred or approved suppliers will already be identified, and perhaps contracted on a standing basis (eg using framework agreements or call-off contracts, whereby the buyer contracts to source its requirements – as and when needed – from the supplier, and purchasers and users can simply 'call off' orders on the agreed terms, as needs arise).

3.2 However, if a new or non-standard item is needed, it will be important to locate, investigate and appraise potential suppliers. The extent of this investigation must be proportionate to the importance and value of the item. It would not be worth the time and cost of detailed supplier appraisal for light bulbs or toilet paper, say. It will be essential, however, for strategic or non-standard items; for major high-value purchases (eg capital equipment); for potential long-term partnership relations with a supplier; and for international sourcing and outsourcing (because of the risks involved).

Survey the market

3.3 'Surveying the market' means identifying or locating suppliers that may potentially be able to supply the requirement. Buyers will constantly be monitoring the supply market(s) relevant to their organisation's requirements, as well as the performance of the existing supplier base. They may also carry out formal supply market research for a given requirement.

3.4 Sources of information about potential suppliers may include: internal records (with existing, past and potential supplier details and performance appraisals); supplier catalogues, sales force presentations and websites; printed and online directories of suppliers and stockists; price comparison websites; online market exchanges or auction sites (such as eBay in the consumer sector); trade or industry exhibitions and conferences; and networking with other buyers (who may be willing to give recommendations and referrals to suppliers with whom they have been satisfied).

3.5 From these preliminary investigations, there may well be a large list of potential suppliers. The next stage then involves:

- Narrowing down the possibilities and
- Accessing or making contact with shortlisted potential suppliers.

3.6 Suppliers may be shortlisted according to a variety of criteria: size or capacity, price, reputation, recommendation – and perhaps the buyer's sustainability policies (eg using small or local suppliers where possible). Potentially interesting suppliers may be contacted by telephone or email to request a brochure or catalogue, a visit to the buyer by the supplier's sales representative, or a visit by the buyer to the supplier.

Appraise (audit) suppliers

3.7 In order to avoid wasting time and resources (for both buyer and supplier), shortlisted potential suppliers should generally be *pre-qualified* before they are invited to quote or tender for a contract: invitations will only be sent to suppliers which the buyer already *knows* to be capable of fulfilling the requirement. This requires the appraisal, evaluation or auditing of potential suppliers.

3.8 A range of criteria may be used to appraise potential suppliers. In an earlier chapter we saw the use of models such as Carter's 10 Cs and the FACE 2 FACE model.

3.9 This information may be acquired by various means: appraisal questionnaires completed by suppliers; perusal of the supplier's financial statements and reports; checking the supplier's certifications, accreditations, quality awards, policy statements and so on; arranging to get references from existing customers; and checking product samples or portfolios of work.

3.10 Once a shortlist of potential suppliers has been identified, the buyer may use a **supplier audit**, **site visit** or **capability survey**: visits to the supplier's premises by a cross-functional appraisal team (eg with experts on procurement, quality and engineering, say) which shares responsibility for the decision to approve or reject the supplier on the basis of their observations.

3.11 Following the appraisal process, one or more suppliers may be officially recognised as being able to meet the standards and requirements of the particular buyer, and therefore eligible for invitations to quote or tender for contracts: this is known as **supplier approval**. The approval may be for a one-off tender, or may mean that the supplier is put on a list of approved suppliers from which user-department purchasers can source products as required.

4 Monitor, review and maintain performance

The purchase-to-pay (P2P) cycle

4.1 Once the contract has been awarded, a new 'cycle' of activity is required to follow it through to completion. This is often called the purchase-to-pay or P2P cycle, but it can be depicted as a two-way flow of transactions as follows: Figure 9.2.

Figure 9.2 *Purchase-to-pay activities*

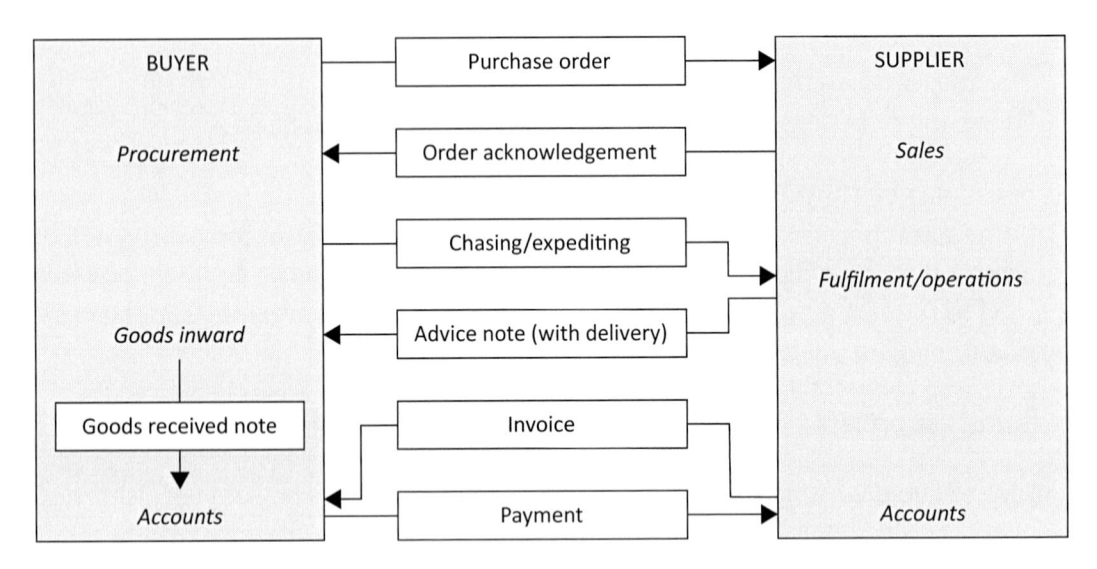

```
        BUYER                                              SUPPLIER
    ┌──────────────┐                                   ┌──────────────┐
    │              │──────── Purchase order ─────────▶│              │
    │  Procurement │◀─────── Order acknowledgement ───│    Sales     │
    │              │                                   │              │
    │              │──────── Chasing/expediting ──────▶│              │
    │              │                                   │ Fulfilment/  │
    │ Goods inward │◀─────── Advice note (with delivery)│ operations  │
    │              │                                   │              │
    │ Goods        │◀─────── Invoice ─────────────────│              │
    │ received note│                                   │              │
    │              │                                   │              │
    │   Accounts   │──────── Payment ─────────────────▶│   Accounts   │
    └──────────────┘                                   └──────────────┘
```

Purchase order and acknowledgement

4.2 For simple purchases, which do not require a negotiated contract, the buyer may make out a *purchase order*: in most cases, a standard form (printed or electronic). The effect of the form will normally be to create a legally binding contract, so it usually contains the firm's standard legal terms and conditions of purchase. In some cases, an order may be placed by phone: usually, where some kind of blanket or 'call off' order system is in place. If not, phone orders should be confirmed in writing, to include the relevant terms and conditions of purchase.

4.3 A number of copies of the purchase order are required, so that appropriate departments can be informed. One copy goes to the supplier (often with a second copy, which can be signed and returned as acknowledgment of the order and acceptance of the legal terms contained on it). One copy will be retained by the procurement department. Other copies may be sent to the stores department, accounts department and user departments, notifying them to await delivery.

Expediting the order

4.4 There will often be a need to follow-up, chase or 'expedite' an order. The buyer may chase the supplier to return the acknowledgment copy of the purchase order, for example, or check that the delivery will be on schedule, or 'track' the progress of the order and its delivery (eg using online 'track and trace' systems, in which each step in the fulfilment of an order, and its transport, is logged for monitoring).

4.5 Usually, these routines are triggered by review of outstanding orders. Most often, purchase orders are logged on a computer system which will automatically flag when follow-up routines are needed.

Goods inwards

4.6 When an order of goods is ready for delivery, a number of routines usually follow in a defined procedure.

- The supplier sends an *advice note* or *delivery note* to the buyer with (or in advance of) delivery of the goods, to notify the buyer of the content and time of the delivery.
- The Goods Inwards department of the buying organisation receives and inspects the goods, to check that the supplier has delivered the correct goods in the correct quantity, without obvious quality defects. The goods must correspond to what was ordered (ie the advice note should correspond to the purchase order).
- The Goods Inwards department sends a *goods received note* (GRN) to the procurement and accounts departments, to indicate that the goods have arrived. This will also indicate any discrepancies or defects in the order, which the procurement department will need to raise and resolve with the supplier, prior to authorisation of payment.

Invoicing and payment

4.7 The supplier will in due course send an invoice or request for payment to the buyer. Procurement should check that it corresponds to the order or contract (in regard to the agreed price) and to the GRN (in regard to goods actually received), and then *either* query discrepancies with the supplier *or* authorise the invoice for payment and pass it to the accounts department for payment.

4.8 Invoices should be paid within the period stated in the agreed terms of trade: often 30, 60 or 90 days. Credit periods are an issue for cashflow, for both the buyer and the supplier. The buyer may want to pay as late as possible, in order to retain his cash (or earn interest on his banked funds), but the supplier will want to be paid as early as possible, to obtain those same benefits – especially since he has already incurred the cost of supplying the product or service.

4.9 It is part of ethical trading to pay supplier invoices *on time, as agreed*. It will impact on the buyer's standing as an attractive (or unattractive) customer for suppliers, and on the ongoing relationship with suppliers. An unjustly unpaid invoice may result in stoppage of supply until the matter is settled, and/or the threat of legal action by the supplier. Repeated late payment or disputed payment of invoices can significantly damage the buyer's credibility, the supplier's loyalty and commitment (and therefore future reliability and quality), and in the worst case, the buyer's ability to find suppliers willing to do business.

4.10 Commercial payments are often made by *electronic credit transfer*, through the banking system, which is safe and swift. (One disadvantage, however, is that payments tend to be handled on regular days of the month, on a payment cycle, which may represent a late payment for a supplier, or prevent the buyer from receiving an early payment discount.)

4.11 Another possibility is payment by *corporate credit card* or *purchasing card*, which allows the delegation of routine purchases to user-department staff, and is efficient in terms of invoicing and other transaction costs. However, this may also allow 'maverick' spending by non-procurement specialists, unless safeguards are in place: eg spending limits on the use of cards, authorised supplier lists and so on.

Contract management

4.12 Contracts for the supply of goods or services may be much more complex, and longer in duration, than a simple purchase order. Once contracts are signed, therefore, it is not as simple as saying: 'The supplier will now do *that*'. There will be obligations to be followed up on either side. If contingencies arise, the contract may (or may not) lay down what happens next. If the supplier's performance falls short in any way, there will be a variety of options for pursuing the matter. Circumstances and requirements may change, and contract terms may have to be adjusted accordingly. This is an ongoing process through the life of the contract – which is where contract management comes in.

4.13 Contract management is the process designed to ensure that both parties to a contract meet their obligations, and that the intended outcomes of a contract are delivered. It also involves building and maintaining a good working relationship between the buyer and supplier, continuing through the life of a contract.

5 Procure-to-pay systems (P2P)

Defining procure to pay (P2P) systems

5.1 Private sector and public sector organisations increasingly face the same pressure to save costs and maximise service delivery. Many organisations have identified that automating the procure-to-pay process is one of the most logical and effective ways of deriving benefits for an organisation. With developments in IT and with increasingly focused software packages these benefits are open to organisations whether they are a large public organisation or a smaller trading company.

5.2 The traditional procure-to-pay process as discussed earlier in this chapter is manually intensive, costly and prone to input errors or delays during the process. Receipt of goods, placing purchase orders, processing purchase invoices, gaining budget holder approval and paying suppliers are all individual areas where delay and error can occur.

5.3 Traditional P2P systems rely on printing information onto pre-printed stationery and posting paper documents. Similarly, when purchase invoices arrive from suppliers they are subject to manually intensive and paper-based internal processes such as recording, approval, coding and storage.

5.4 All the above factors, linked with the increasing use of IT both within individual organisations and increasingly as companies link IT systems, have served to drive the development of the practical application of P2P systems in recent years.

5.5 Procure-to-pay systems enable the procurement function to be integrated with the accounts payable function. P2P systems are proven to be effective and practical for many organisations. P2P systems incorporate the following activities.

- Supply management
- Requisition
- Purchase order
- Receiving
- Invoice reconciliation
- Accounts payable

5.6 CIPS define P2P as 'a seamless process enabled by technology designed to speed up the process from point of order to payment'.

5.7 A further definition used by SAP (the software company) is 'the P2P process contains all the steps from purchasing goods from a supplier, to paying the supplier'.

Automating requisitions, purchase orders and invoices

5.8 The automation of the P2P process can lead to better financial controls, lower production costs, reduced overheads and better and more efficient relationships with operations staff and suppliers.

5.9 The goal of P2P programs is to automate processes by introducing efficiency controls. This involves the application of controls such as cross-referencing procurement budgets with pre-defined buying limits, ensuring that approval limits are met before progressing the order or ensuring that product specifications are consistent throughout the purchase cycle. These controls are the result of detailed discussions with Internet or software suppliers or consultants at the introductory phase of P2P and are designed to deliver a system suitable both for the individual business and for integration with outside companies as appropriate.

5.10 There are four distinct phases within the P2P process, each involving different documents.

- Communication with suppliers using purchase orders and remittance advices
- Data capture from supplier documents such as purchase orders and remittance advices
- Authorisation and coding of internal documents
- Making the payment

Communication with suppliers

5.11 Moving away from pre-printed stationery can be seen as the first step in reducing document production costs. Desktop publishing tools can be used to provide a consistent layout for documents while giving the ability to adapt or introduce flexibility by varying details or terms and conditions to suit individual circumstances without compromising the overall system. Such flexibility will be subject to pre-incorporated approvals.

5.12 While plain paper printing gives the most cost effective print solution it becomes evident that greater savings and efficiencies can be gained through the electronic delivery of documents.

5.13 Email allows for prompt recordable communication at low cost. Merging a document into the email as a PDF attachment is becoming increasingly standard. Once the process of creation and distribution of documents has been automated the organisation can look at the delivery of relevant documents linked to the transaction both internally and externally as required.

5.14 Copies of documents may need to be stored for several years. Efficient archiving can be built into the system at an early stage allowing these obligations to be met with the required documents stored electronically.

Data capture

5.15 The control of in-house documents and their accompanying data is only one part of the process. The links with outside organisations (such as suppliers) must operate effectively in order to provide the required information to the system in a timely manner.

5.16 With internal documents an organisation will have the originating data but this is not the case with external supplier documents. In order to process this data organisations will typically have to re-key this information into their own finance systems. This is time-consuming and prone to error.

5.17 The automation of this process is an important step. Optical character recognition (OCR) can be used to capture key data. Unique data such as the company's registration number can identify the supplier and information can then be extracted and validated before being progressed further.

Authorisation and coding

5.18 When an invoice has been processed by the finance operation there is usually a requirement for internal budget holders to approve the purchase invoice for payment and/or to allocate to particular budgets. Internal operations can benefit from using an electronic authorisation process where an email can be sent to the appropriate person indicating they have a task to complete. The link in the email will provide detail and present a copy of the invoice and relevant support information allowing the authorised person to input the required budget codes and authorise or query.

5.19 Once given final approval, the data can be automatically imported into the P2P system to update the status of the purchase invoice. We will examine approvals further in the following section.

Making the payment

5.20 With the purchase invoice transaction approved and coded the purchase is on the system awaiting payment. Traditionally payments were made by cheque and this method is still used, particularly by smaller companies. However increasingly payments via automated bank transfer are viewed as the most cost-effective method. This system ensures security of payment coupled with an electronic record of payment.

5.21 Batches of payments are raised, and validated against known account codes before requiring a digital signature to approve the payment. The digital signature is provided by a secure chip and pin system. Payment reports are available electronically and can help in identifying if any errors or mistakes in payment have been made. If they have, they can be rectified.

E-sourcing

5.22 E-sourcing is defined as 'using the internet to make decisions and form strategies regarding how and where services or products are obtained' (*CIPS*): in other words, using electronic tools for the pre-contract or 'sourcing' part of the procurement cycle.

- **E-catalogues:** suppliers exhibit their products in electronic catalogues, which can be viewed online or downloaded by potential purchasers
- **E-tendering**, using e-RFQs (electronic requests for quotation) and specifications posted online or emailed to potential suppliers. Bids can also be received and evaluated electronically against pre-set criteria.

- **E-auctions**, conducted online using the buyer's or seller's website, or third-party auction sites such as eBay.
- **Market exchanges**: sites where multiple buyers and sellers meet to exchange goods.
- **Online supplier evaluation data**: third party reports, customer feedback, registers and directories of approved or accredited suppliers, benchmarking reports, market intelligence tools and so on
- **Requirement planning and specification tools**. Examples include integrated systems for resource planning (eg materials requirements planning) and design and development systems (eg computer aided design and manufacture – CAD/CAM)

E-procurement

5.23 E-procurement is the follow-up to e-sourcing: the application of information and communication technology to the later part of the procurement cycle. All stages of the P2P cycle can be computerised, with tools such as the following.

- *Desk-top procurement systems*: allowing users to call off stock electronically
- *Electronic data interchange (EDI)*: direct exchange of documents, in standardised electronic form, between linked computers in a buyer-supplier network
- *Online track-and-trace*: global positioning systems using barcodes or radio frequency identification (RFID) to track deliveries and goods in storage, linked to transport planning and inventory systems which can 'flag' problems for expediting
- *Payment*: automated invoice/order matching; electronic invoice generation; electronic funds transfer; and the use of purchasing cards
- *Contract management systems*: updating electronic contracts for changes; reporting by exception on performance discrepancies and so on.
- *Database information*: eg supplier performance data (captured and updated in real time).

Requisitioning

5.24 P2P can be viewed as a stage-based process as individual stages have to be completed before progress can be made. Unless predetermined criteria are met (or overridden) the transaction will not be permitted to proceed. An early stage in the process is the production of a requisition.

5.25 Requisitions are generated by operations staff looking to purchase goods or services. In manual environments these will be completed on paper or in some cases telephoned to the supplier directly. Automating the process brings control from the outset.

5.26 The requisition is a formal request to purchase something such as inventory material, office supplies, services etc, needed by the organisation. They can only be created by an employee.

5.27 By automating the requisitioning function a set methodology is put in place for staff to request goods and services electronically. Options may include requisitioning by repeat order, blanket order, via a catalogue or a template of items that the purchaser is authorised to order or by other methods permitted by the system.

5.28 The issuer of the requisition will require approval before the purchase can be made. In the manual environment this will usually require completion of a form that needs to be authorised by someone more senior in the organisation. This is both time-consuming and prone to delay. By automating the process the requisition can be approved either automatically with set limits or via email, allowing for both a faster response and accurate record keeping.

5.29 The P2P system will automatically check procurement budgets to ensure compliance with predetermined buying limits. Requisitions that pass up-front validation are automatically routed for approval to appropriate individuals, who can view a requisition's history, amend or reject the requisition, attach supporting documents and return the requisition to the originator, or approve and release the requisition

Issuing purchase orders

5.30 Once the requisition has been approved the purchase order can be issued to the supplier. Again, in a manual environment orders will be telephoned or possibly faxed to suppliers. Within a P2P system purchase orders are issued electronically, increasing accuracy and enabling electronic acknowledgments from the supplier.

Receiving goods and services

5.31 An integral part of the P2P system is the knowledge that goods or services have been delivered to the right place at the right time and in the right quantity and condition. Manual feedback can be error-prone and subject to delay. By ensuring goods and service receipt is acknowledged electronically in a predetermined manner the system can complete this stage or recognise that part of the order remains outstanding before progressing further.

Receiving invoices

5.32 Within a manual environment many accounts departments continue to process a large volume of paper invoices. Within a developed P2P system invoices can be received electronically through EDI, electronic invoicing and other methods. Invoices that are received manually can be scanned and the relevant data captured, creating a fully electronic environment.

Matching invoices

5.33 Following receipt, invoices should be matched to purchase orders and receipts in order that the invoice paid is based on the actual goods received at the negotiated price. P2P will automatically perform a three way match (invoice, receipt, and purchase order) to ensure that only matched invoices are eligible for payment. The system will automatically re-route mismatches to the appropriate users for review and resolution.

Issuing payments

5.34 Payment by cheque is becoming less common. Payment via online banking services, credit and debit cards, and purchases via purchasing cards all serve to provide control and accurate record keeping. As such these systems integrate well with P2P systems.

Creating approvals and their timescales

5.35 With manual systems in procurement it is necessary for someone in a more senior position to authorise the purchase decision of a subordinate. It may be that certain products or spend limits are automatically authorised but generally it has long been considered good practice to ensure purchase decisions are approved by a more senior person or by a specialist person.

5.36 This logic also applies to P2P systems. Decisions made will usually require some form of authorisation before they are allowed to proceed. Depending on the size and complexity of the organisation this process can become highly involved and in consequence developing an 'approval hierarchy' forms a key part of P2P systems.

5.37 An approval hierarchy is a private hierarchy within an organisation that allows authorised individuals to approve purchase and financial transactions. It is important to note that only one approval hierarchy should exist within the P2P system (similar hierarchies may exist in other business disciplines, notably IT and HR).

5.38 An approval hierarchy will contain various approval levels that funnel transaction approval up through an approval chain. At each level the authorised individual can approve or reject the submitted transaction.

5.39 Here is an example of how it works. In this example the Senior Manager is the manager of the Junior Buyer and the Group Manager is the manager of the Senior Manager.

EMPLOYEE	IS MANAGED BY	APPROVAL LIMIT ($)
Junior Buyer	Senior Manager	50.00
Senior Manager	Group Manager	100.00
Group Manager		Unlimited

- The Junior Buyer raises a purchase order that has a total value of $150.00.
- The purchase order is submitted for approval.
- As the Junior Buyer does not have high enough approval limits, the purchase order is automatically forwarded to the senior manager (as the Senior Manager is the Junior Buyer's supervisor as defined in the hierarchy).
- The Senior Manager responds to the approval notification for this purchase order.
- If the Senior Manager selects 'Approve' the purchase order is automatically forwarded to the Group Manager as the Senior Buyer does not have a high enough approval limit.
- The purchase order appears on the notification screen for the Group Manager where it can be approved or rejected.

Resolving queries and anomalies

5.40 To ensure procurement timescales are being met it is necessary to incorporate within the P2P process a hierarchy to ensure queries and anomalies are dealt with promptly and efficiently. Identified anomalies are emailed to the relevant approver for resolution. The nominated approver can then forward, hold, reject or approve the invoice. Many systems will send email alerts with automatic escalations built in to ensure that the anomaly is quickly dealt with, and invoices or queries do not get lost in approvers' inboxes.

5.41 The system places pressure on the approver to resolve the situation in a timely manner by recording the time of the original notification and automatically escalating the query perhaps to remind the approver or to advise the next person higher up the hierarchy that a query still exists after a set time.

5.42 In certain cases it may be prudent to have a person outside the hierarchy to review the situation. A reviewer is an individual outside the approver's hierarchy to whom a requisition or anomaly has been forwarded for review. A reviewer does not have any approval authority. Instead their views will be recorded in the approval history with their review comments only.

6 Integration of systems between organisations

6.1 As we have discussed, the traditional view of the procurement cycle has been impacted heavily over recent years by new technology. One area that has seen considerable growth is the integration of systems among organisations.

6.2 Any business that has invested in technology over a period of years is likely to find itself with a number of different systems and software programs that may prove incompatible with each other over time. The order process system may not talk to the accounts software, the forecasting system may not link to the procurement system, and so on. Systems can in many ways hinder as well as support business objectives.

6.3 Larger organisations have been able to view IT differently. Many have looked at installing and supporting an enterprise resource planning system (ERP) since they were first developed in the mid 1990s. These systems provide an integrated approach to all the component parts of an organisation's business.

6.4 ERP systems have also been important in the integration of IT systems *between* organisations. With investment by the major hardware and software developers linked to the rapid growth of IT capability what seemed unlikely ten years ago is now a reality for many small and medium sized enterprises – the ability to integrate systems between organisations. Specialist systems integration companies now provide services to meet the needs of smaller organisations.

The benefits

6.5 The concept behind integration is simple: the whole can be greater than the sum of the parts. The more systems and processes link together, the greater the overall benefit.

6.6 Integrated systems are viewed as more agile and responsive in the way they operate. Linking with other companies or bodies allows them to streamline their operation by improving the flow of information between companies, meeting the needs of companies they interlink with and often being viewed as a business partner over the long term.

6.7 Here are some of the principal benefits.
- Improved efficiency. Integrated systems give greater accuracy and reduce waste as they allow organisations to operate using real-time figures rather than estimates. Production can be linked to ordering; procurement can be linked to finance; and so on.
- Improved job satisfaction. Staff morale improves as integration reduces administration and allows staff to focus on the more skilled aspects of their job. Linked systems benefit as information is better, reducing frustration and helping to improve work-rates.
- Competitive advantage. Integration places an organisation in a strong position to improve relationships with customers and suppliers. Many businesses will collaborate on forecasts and procurement with suppliers, or give customers direct access to certain levels of their systems. In turn other companies will reciprocate by allowing similar interrogation of their systems.

Integration options

6.8 Organisations looking to integrate systems need to decide on the best approach for them and their future business needs. This section examines some of the technical solutions available.

6.9 An **integration hub** is a method of linking processes and systems gradually. In essence it is a system that sits between existing systems and enables the systems to talk to one another. This comes from the fact that many organisations have developed IT systems in a piecemeal manner, making the best decisions at the time but perhaps failing to consider the future needs of the business. As an example, accounting packages such as Sage can be integrated with orders, procurement and stock demands.

6.10 The benefit of an integration hub is that there is no requirement to replace all the existing systems. Some hubs use XML (extensible mark-up language) as a way of formatting data which then allows information to be shared across different platforms and across the web.

6.11 A **hosted solution** allows you to rent integration services over the internet from application service providers (ASPs). The software is hosted and maintained by the ASP as a form of outsourcing. This approach can be seen as more flexible than an integration hub, with support and upgrades forming an integral part of the contract. As with any outsourced contract you will be heavily reliant on the provider which may prove problematic if you decide to end the contract.

6.12 **Systems integrators** are individuals or businesses that build computing systems for clients by combining hardware and software products from multiple vendors. Using a systems integrator, a company can align cheaper, pre-configured components and off-the-shelf software to meet key business goals, as opposed to more expensive, customised implementations that may require original programming or manufacture of unique components. Creation of these information systems may include designing or building customised architecture, integrating it with new or existing hardware, packaged and custom software, and communications infrastructure.

6.13 **Solutions providers** are the big software players such as SAP and Oracle that build bespoke integration solutions based on their own proprietary software. With their own software widely accepted across industry this solution is highly suitable for those organisations wishing to develop a fully integrated system with the ability to be controlled and maintained in-house.

6.14 This provides a powerful, industry-standard, robust solution but comes at a high price. Solutions providers have tended to be used by listed companies and larger organisations but new products have been developed over recent years that now makes this option more attractive to the SME sector.

Chapter summary

- The procurement cycle is a list of stages in a typical purchase transaction, beginning with identification of a need and ending with contract award and subsequent performance monitoring.
- Identification of a need is usually signalled by a purchase requisition or a bill of materials.
- It is normal to identify and pre-qualify potential suppliers. Use of Carter's 10Cs or the FACE 2 FACE model can help in this process.
- Later stages of the procurement cycle include the purchase order, expediting, goods inwards procedures, invoicing, payment and contract management.
- Nowadays, many or all of the stages in the cycle are automated.
- Automation now typically extends beyond the boundaries of a single firm. It is common for different firms within a supply chain to integrate their electronic systems.

Self-test questions

Numbers in brackets refer to paragraphs where you can check your answers.

1. List the stages in the procurement cycle. (Figure 9.1)
2. List some of the key forms and documents involved in a procurement transaction. (1.7)
3. List details included on a typical purchase requisition form. (2.4)
4. Give examples of sources of information about potential suppliers. (3.4)
5. Describe a typical Goods Inwards procedure. (4.6)
6. Define (a) e-sourcing, and (b) e-procurement. (5.22, 5.23)
7. Explain how invoices are vouched for payment in an electronic P2P system. (5.33)
8. What are the benefits of systems integration along the supply chain? (6.7)

CHAPTER 10

Internet Technologies in Procurement

Assessment criteria and indicative content

2.3 Assess approaches to the sourcing of supplies
- The use of e-sourcing technologies

3.2 Explain how the use of internet technologies can support procurement operations
- Providing data to smooth demand and supply
- Communicating via the internet
- Web-based solutions such as e-requisitioning, e-sourcing, e-ordering, e-invoicing

Section headings

1. IT and procurement
2. Communicating via the internet
3. Web-based solutions
4. Data to smooth demand and supply

Introduction

Procurement is an information function. It needs good information to function well, and it is an important provider of strategic and operational information.

In this chapter, we look at the impact of information technology on management of organisations and on the procurement function in particular and consider how the evolution of the procurement function has been supported by technological developments.

1 IT and procurement

The evolution of procurement

1.1 *Baily et al* describe the historical development of the procurement function in terms of its information systems technology.

- **Infant stage**: a simple manual clerical system, supporting operational decision-making within the procurement department.
- **Awakening stage**: improvement of the manual system, and exploration of early standalone computer processing, in response to the recognition of the importance of information to support procurement decisions.
- **Developing stage**: beginning to link procurement IT systems with those of other functions, to support more integrated materials planning and management.

- **Mature stage**: full computerisation of procurement information processing within the firm, with an integrated procurement database supporting coordinated materials planning and management.
- **Advanced stage**: direct EDI link of internal procurement database to the external supply chain (key customers and suppliers), for full integration of supply processes, efficiency of transaction processing and enhancement of supply chain relationships.

Computerisation of procurement systems

1.2 Computerised information systems have transformed administrative work in all areas. They offer the following key benefits for procurement.

- Routine and repetitive clerical tasks are automated, requiring less time and effort from buyers, who are free to spend more time on the creative, strategic and relational aspects of their roles.
- Information storage and retrieval is less wasteful of physical space and resources, and of clerical time. Computer disks and CDs can store massive amounts of information safely, cleanly and in a very small physical space. Cloud systems allow storage offsite very easily. Records can be interactively interrogated, updated and transmitted without generating extra paper products.
- Data can be manipulated faster and more flexibly, for a range of transaction and decision-support functions.

1.3 An article in *Supply Management* cited the example of UK supermarket giant Sainsbury's, which over several years completely re-engineered its supply chain. Among other changes (involving the structure of the distribution system), Sainsbury's fully automated its warehouses, in order to minimise human error and implement zero defect order fulfilment. It also introduced real-time information and collaborative commerce across the extended supply chain. This included:

- computerised inventory management, to enhance control by Sainsbury's over the supplier-to-store replenishment network;
- data-mining applications, gathering information at point of sale, measuring on-shelf availability on an hour-by-hour basis, and facilitating real-time reordering.

1.4 You should be aware of computerised applications through your studies of procurement procedures and processes: materials and inventory management, purchase requisitions and orders, order expediting and delivery tracking, electronic payments, budgetary control and other management reports.

2 Communicating via the internet

2.1 The growth of online communication tools has had a profound impact on the communication process.

2.2 Effective communication forms an essential part of a smoothly running business. Communication involves the transmission of information from a source (or sources) to a receiver (or receivers). The information is communicated in the form of a message.

2.3 In modern business there will be multi-channel flows of communication. For example a customer may request a new part from a supplier, along with information on how to use it. The supplier will then communicate with the customer, sending out instructions for using the part, as well as a delivery note, invoice and further sales literature.

2.4 Increasingly these interactions are carried out by electronic means through a website, email or other means of communication. The effectiveness of communications depends on the following factors.

- The clarity of the message
- The quality of the medium used to transmit the message (for example email, telephone, text message, letter etc)
- Any distracting 'noise' that prevents the message from getting through. For example, if the recipient receives lots of email messages he may fail to give the proper attention to the sender's message
- The ability of the receiver to 'decode' the message. For example, they may not be able to understand the instructions given.

2.5 There are two main forms of business communications: internal communication (within the business) and external communication (communication outside the business).

Internal communication

2.6 Here are some typical forms of internal communication.

- Email. This has rapidly become the most common form of written communication within organisations.
- Company websites. A website will typically involve a portal or section dedicated to internal communication with and between employees.
- Company databases. In most large organisations employees will be able to access a number of company databases (for example, to access details of customer accounts when dealing directly with customers).
- Face-to-face interactions. Dealing directly with other employees in an organisation is a regular occurrence and provides an excellent way for sharing ideas and for working co-operatively.
- Meetings can either be formal or informal in nature. In many companies teams of employees regularly meet to discuss issues about quality.
- Phone communications are another important form of oral communication with most large companies having a low cost internal telephone system.
- An internal memo (memorandum) is a brief message to another member of the same organisation. Typically memos today are sent by email.
- Staff magazines, notices and posters on staff notice boards provide other means of internal communications.

2.7 Here are some typical forms of external communication.

- Written communication in the form of letters, and advertising material such as leaflets, brochures, posters, etc
- Press releases
- Reports to government and other agencies
- Oral communication in the form of phone calls
- Web-based communications including email and video conferencing
- Websites.

3 Web-based solutions

3.1 Web-based communication enables you to integrate data directly into the system of a business partner using the traditional communication through telephone or email. In this way, new forms of business relationships arise. Consumers or business partners can communicate with a partner system via web applications. Here are some examples.

- Email. This is the simplest method of communication where an individual can address and transmit a message to one or more specific other individuals recognised by their email address. Email on the internet is not routed through any central control point, and can take numerous and varying paths to recipients. Email can be accessed or viewed on intermediate computers and other devices between the sender and recipient (unless the message is encrypted).
- Instant messaging. AIM Pro is the business class version of instant messaging which integrates with Microsoft Outlook, desktop and file sharing, with access to WebEx meetings.
- Video conferencing. This is long-established and there are many providers. Video conferencing enables parties from different parts of the country or other countries to attend the same meeting where they can contribute and listen in a similar manner to being at the meeting.

3.2 When companies integrate systems one major benefit is that the two or more organisations effectively become just one. When those benefits are combined with the power of the world wide web supported by constantly updated software there are tremendous opportunities for building businesses.

3.3 One of the most visible impacts of web-based solutions is in areas such as online conferences, meetings, business development showcases and training which can be made highly professional, focused and cost-effective via internet delivery.

3.4 The world wide web provides the opportunity to create one-to-one interactive relationships across the entire range of business disciplines linking down to individual customers if required.

3.5 The introduction of an e-procurement system has been identified as a mechanism for many companies to improve their procurement processes and thereby reduce the cost of procurement and deliver better value for money. E-procurement is the use of secure web-based platforms to communicate with bidders in a paperless environment, free from inconveniences, delays, and physical insecurities of any kind.

3.6 The phrase e-procurement can cover a number of elements.

- The ability to download bidding documents from a website
- Submission of bids through an electronic tender box
- The development of management information systems to assist with procurement reporting as well as oversight and monitoring
- The ability to initiate reverse auctions
- The incorporation of the systems of 'procure-to-pay' in interactions with suppliers and others

3.7 Web-based solutions are constantly evolving. As the capabilities of the web improves and as the software improves the potential for both organisations and governments is huge. Correctly managed, and with an eye on the future, web-based solutions are a key business consideration for the present and future growth of any organisation.

3.8 For detailed topics such as e-requisitioning, e-sourcing, e-ordering and e-invoicing, you should refer back to the previous chapter.

4 Data to smooth demand and supply

Forecasting supply and demand

4.1 The management of supply and demand is a major issue in business management. For the manufacturing organisation, accurate forecasting brings improved control over stock management. This helps with reducing costs, improving scheduling of manufacture and providing customers with a better level of customer service. For the service organisation, where physical stock delivery may not be the main criterion, operational demand can be viewed and delivered against service-orientated criteria such as service level agreements and/or key performance indicators.

4.2 The need to assess demand accurately is crucial in today's business environment. Accuracy in forecasting brings with it the opportunity to maximise resources and minimise spend and waste. The increased business emphasis in forecasting and demand management marks it out as an identified aspect of business operations where substantial gains can be made and competitive advantage enhanced.

4.3 Confidence in the predictability of supply and demand and the data that supports the predictability enables better decisions to be made particularly at the operational level. When accurate forecasting is linked to effective inventory management the two areas combine to be greater than the sum of their parts.

4.4 Demand is not as predictable as organisations would like. Product lifecycles are shorter, customer demands are greater and may require increasing flexibility, and competition is fiercer. Traditional inventory management systems for dependent demand items (where the demand for one particular product is directly related to another product) have tended to look at established systems such as MRP which are designed to minimise stockholding within accepted limits while also looking to maximise production efficiencies by accurately forecasting future demand.

4.5 Forecasting has a key role to play in ensuring resources are available when needed and so is the operational flexibility to meet demand if forecasts do not prove to be totally correct. Accurate prediction of supply and demand enables better ordering, scheduling and capacity mananagement. It reduces waste and can give a commercial advantage that competitors may struggle to match.

4.6 Forecasting is an essential part of all planning and decision-making and is of fundamental importance to many areas of business operations. Forecasting provides a crucial element in the business planning process and, in consequence, is the focus of considerable attention to organisations.

4.7 Accurate forecasting can mean that the right resources are available as required. Inaccurate forecasting can mean remedying operational activities to bring them in line with strategic plans. Forecasts will rarely be 100% accurate as they are based on projections and assumptions. Traditionally forecasts are categorised as long-term, medium-term and short-term.

- Long-term forecasts are usually for a two to five year time period but can extend to ten or twenty years in certain industries such as mining, oil or when major manufacturing plants are being built.

- Medium-term forecasts have a time scale of six months to two years. For the operations manager these forecasts are important as they allow for consideration of investment decisions or issues such as subcontracting.
- Short-term forecasts have a time scale often shorter than six months. The relevance of these forecasts to the operations manager is that they become a relevant planning tool that enables the twin goals of effectiveness and efficiency to be implemented. The shorter the time frame the more accurate the forecast should be.

4.8 Forecasting is often a combination of 'hard data' (ie facts and figures such as prices, trends, sales etc) and 'soft data' (eg customer feedback, market knowledge etc). The majority of forecasts rely on hard data for the basis of the forecast with soft data being applied as assumptions during the forecasting project or at the presentation stage where the assumptions and soft data applied should be fully discussed.

Internet technologies in forecasting

4.9 Business forecasting involves a wide range of tools including simple spreadsheets, enterprise resource planning (ERP) systems, electronic data interchange networks (EDI), advanced supply chain management systems, and other web-enabled technologies. The practice of business forecasting attempts to pinpoint key factors in business production and extrapolate from given data sets to produce accurate projects for future costs, revenues and opportunities.

4.10 Forecasting systems draw on many sources of data for their forecasting input including databases, emails, documents, and websites. For forecasts to provide information to smooth out demand and supply it will be necessary to examine the data on factors such as consumer trends, seasonality, advertising effectiveness for demand and commodity prices, shipping issues and market trends.

4.11 Companies have a vast array of business forecasting systems and software from which to choose. According to the *Journal of Business Forecasting Methods & Systems*, any forecasting system needs to be able to facilitate data-sharing partnerships between businesses, accept input from several different data sources and platforms, operate on an open architecture, and feature an array of analysis techniques and approaches.

Capacity management strategies

4.12 Capacity management is concerned with ensuring that the capacity of the operation matches the evolving demands of the business in the most effective and time efficient manner. The aim of capacity management is to strike a balance between:

- *Cost and capacity:* to ensure that any processing capacity purchased is justifiable in terms of both business need and the efficient use of resources.
- *Supply and demand:* making sure that the availability of goods or services matches the demands made on the business.

4.13 Capacity management deals with the identification of present and future business requirements in order to ensure that demand needs are met cost effectively. The more accurate forecasting is, the easier it is to manage capacity. There are two main strategies for capacity management.

- *Capacity leading demand:* here capacity is designed to be able to produce more goods or services than the forecast demand. The operation should then have enough capacity to meet anticipated demand. This ensures that revenue is maximised and that customer satisfaction

standards are high. This approach also means that the operation will operate with a certain amount of 'slack' built in to meet increases in demand and as a result the utilisation of the operational capability may be low.
- *Capacity lagging demand:* here capacity will not meet the demand anticipated of it. This ensures that resources will have a high degree of utilisation but may still be insufficient to meet anticipated demand, causing customer dissatisfaction.

Smoothing capacity

4.14 Where possible organisations will endeavour to have demand fluctuations smoothed out or eliminated altogether. There are various techniques to achieve this such as offering inducements to customers (such as price reductions, additional quantities etc) which may advance demand. Although profit margins may be affected, the exercise may be cost effective as the operation keeps running and the product being manufactured may offer the least reduction in profit margin.

4.15 Encouraging customers to wait for completion of their orders will clearly affect customer service levels and the reputation of the organisation. It requires careful handling and management. Subcontracted manufacture may be utilised to meet peaks in demand but this approach may cause issues as contractual agreements will be entered into, specifications agreed and quality standards established and monitored among a range of other related issues.

4.16 Spare capacity may be used to build up stock that can be used or sold at a later date. Finished stock bears not only the delivery price of the component parts but also the cost of the transformation process that goes into the finished item. Holding finished inventory ties up capital. There is also a risk that the stock may deteriorate or become obsolete.

The role of procurement in providing data

4.17 The procurement function of any organisation has an operational role that connects it directly to suppliers. Suppliers are an important source of both hard and soft data when examined from a forecasting standpoint. Their knowledge of their particular market provides the purchaser with an opportunity to gather up-to-date information on trends or issues that may impact on the supplier's ability to deliver, price trends in the supplier's industry etc.

4.18 This is not a new area to many in procurement. Many buyers gather information through discussions with suppliers and use it to make decisions or pass on the knowledge to those in their organisation who would benefit. As the scope of procurement is now so wide in many organisations this knowledge needs to be captured and entered onto a computer based system for dissemination throughout the organisation and to provide both hard and soft data for the purpose of forecasting.

4.19 Many software programs provide the purchaser with the opportunity to input this type of data. This information is both current and credible and is of considerable value to an organisation and its supply chain partners.

4.20 In isolation one piece of information may be of little value but when viewed across an organisation it can provide an important contribution to accurate forecasting which in turn should lead to more effective production or service delivery.

Chapter summary

- Technology has transformed the work of procurement professionals, in particular by freeing up time previously spent on routine and repetitive clerical tasks.
- The internet is a powerful communication tool.
- Web-based communications include email, instant messaging and video conferencing.
- Forecasting is a key technique for procurement professionals. Accurate advance knowledge of demand enables buyers to plan procurement and production effectively.

Self-test questions

Numbers in brackets refer to paragraphs where you can check your answers.

1. List the stages in IT development identified by Baily et al. (1.1)
2. What are the benefits of computerised procurement systems for buyers? (1.2)
3. List some forms of internal and external communication. (2.6, 2.7)
4. Suggest likely time frames for short-term, medium-term and long-term forecasts. (4.7)
5. Suggest methods of smoothing production capacity. (4.14)
6. Explain the role of procurement in the provision of forecast data. (4.17–4.20)

Subject Index

ABC analysis 55
Absorption costing 26
Achieved savings. 30
Achieving quality supplies 35
Acknowledgement of order. 130
Acquisition costs of inventory 57
Added value 4
Added value, role of procurement 6
Added value negotiating 20
Analysing quotations and tenders. 29
Appraisal costs 40
Approvals and their timescales 136
Approved suppliers. 44, 129
Authorisation and coding of orders. 134
Automating requisitions. 133

Barcodes 61
Bill of materials. 128
Budgetary constraints. 78
Buffer stocks 57
Buyer's role in specification 75

Capability survey. 107, 129
Capacity management 146
Carter's 10Cs. 105
Communicating via the internet 142
Communication with suppliers 133
Competition and quotations 27
Competitive bidding. 27
Computerisation of procurement systems. . . 142
Conformance specification 37, 88
Continuous improvement 49
Contract administration 116
Contract management. 68, 116, 132
Contracts. 113
Contribution pricing 22
Corporate social responsibility 3, 104
Cost analysis 18
Cost behaviour 25
Cost reduction strategy 8
Cost savings. 7, 32
Cost transparency. 18, 26
Cost-based pricing 21
Costs of inventory. 54
Costs of quality 40
Creating specifications 85
Crosby, Philip. 46
Cross-functional specification development 72

Data capture 134
Data to smooth demand and supply. 145
Defect detection 44
Defect prevention. 45
Delivery performance. 66
Delphi method 59
Deming, W Edwards. 43
Dependent and independent demand 58
Design specifications 89
Development of specifications 76, 79
Dimensions of quality. 36
Direct and indirect costs. 24
Distributive bargaining. 19
Document management 117

Early buyer involvement. 75
Early supplier involvement. 44, 76
E-auctions 120
Economic order quantity 62
Efficiency and effectiveness 6, 31
Electronic P2P 125
Environmental management systems. 104
E-procurement 135
E-sourcing 134
Ethics 3
Expediting 68, 130
Expert opinion. 59
Exponential smoothing 59
External failure costs 41
External lead time. 65

Face2Face 106
Failure mode and effect analysis. 46
Financial appraisal of suppliers 108
Fitness for purpose. 37
Five rights of procurement. 1
Fixed and variable costs 25
Fixed order quantity system. 62
Forecasting demand. 58, 145
Formation of agreements 113
Framework agreement. 27
Functional specification 92

Good practice 4
Goods inwards 131

Historical data on prices. 18
Holding costs of inventory 57

Identifying needs	71, 127	P2P systems	125, 132
Implied terms in contracts	115	Pareto, Vilfredo	55
Importance of specifications	86	Paying suppliers	134
Improving performance	117	Penetration pricing	21
Information on suppliers	100	Performance measurement	32, 110
Information requirements for specifications	76	Performance specification	37, 88, 92
Innovation	3	Periodic review system	60
Inspection for quality control	45	Perpetual inventory	61
Integration of systems between organisations	138	Planning milestones and activities	66
Integrative bargaining	20	Porter's value chain	5
Internal communication	143	Pre-qualification of suppliers	101
Internal failure costs	41	Prevention costs	40
Internal lead time	64	Price	15
Internet technologies	141	Price analysis	17
Inventory costs	54	Price discrimination	22
Inventory management	55	Price/cost iceberg	7
Invoicing and payment	131	Pricing decisions	20
Ishikawa diagrams	47	Pricing strategies	21
Ishikawa, Kaoru	49	Primary and secondary activities	5
ISO14000	104	Procurement, evolution of	141
ISO9000	48, 103	Procurement cycle	126
		Procurement effectiveness	31
Juran, Joseph	37	Procurement efficiency	31
Just in time supply	60	Procurement functionality	31
		Procurement needs	71
Kaizen	49	Procurement price	16
Key performance indicators	67, 94	Products and services	10
		Promotional pricing	22
Late customisation	55	Psychological pricing	22
Lead times	64, 78	Purchase orders	130
Legislation and specifications	80	Purchase requisitions	127
Liaison with users and customers	71	Push and pull strategies	59
Linking costs and prices	23		
		Quality, defining	36
Make or buy decision	81	Quality assurance	43, 45
Managing delivery performance	66	Quality circles	49
Managing supplier quality	42	Quality control	42, 44
Marginal costing	26	Quality management	43
Market skimming	21	Quality management systems	43, 47
Market-based pricing	21	Quality of supplies	35
Marketing research	59	Quality related costs	40
Measuring achieved savings	30	Quality standards	47
Measuring delivery performance	67	Queries and anomalies in P2P	137
Measuring supplier performance	110	Queries and clarifications	118
Minimum order quantities	55	Quotations from suppliers	27
Mistakes in tenders	121		
Modified re-buy	126	Radio frequency identification	61
		Reducing lead times	66
Negotiating improved prices	19	Regression analysis	59
New buy	126	Relationship development	2
		Re-order level	62
Obtaining supplies	1	Request for quotation	27
Open book costing	26	Requisitions	127, 135
Open tendering	28	Reverse auctions	120
Order acknowledgement	130	Reviewing needs from customers	73
Output/outcome-based specifications	88	Right price	15
Overheads	24	Right quality	36
		Right quantity	53
		Right time	53, 64

Safety stocks	57
Sales price	16
Schedules and lead times	78
Scheduling	59
Second bids in tenders	122
Selective tendering	28
Service gaps	39
Service level agreements	11
Service quality	38
Services, features of	10
Services, specification of	93
SERVQUAL model	38
Simple moving average	59
Site visits	107, 129
SMART objectives	94
Smoothing capacity	147
Sources of added value	5
Sources of supplier information	100
Sourcing of supplies	99
Specification by brand name	90
Specification by market grade	91
Specification by properties	89
Specification by sample	90
Specification by standards	91
Specification development	74, 76, 79
Specification failure	42
Specifications and contracts	86
Specifications	37, 85
Specifications, definition of	71
Specifying services	93
Stages of sourcing process	126
Stakeholders in procurement	80
Statistical process control	45
Straight re-buy	126
Suboptimal decisions	8
Supplier appraisal	101, 129

Supplier approval	129
Supplier audit	129
Supplier certification	43
Supplier database	100
Supplier delivery performance	66
Supplier development	44
Supplier management	94
Supplier questionnaires	107
Supplier's cost base	24
Supplier's role in specification	76
Suppliers' approaches to pricing	20
Surveying the market	99, 128
Technical specifications	89
Tendering	27
Terms of contracts	113
Time series analysis	59
Tolerances	85
Total acquisition cost	7
Total cost of ownership	3, 7
Total lead time	65
Total quality management	43, 48
Trade-offs in the five rights	3
Transition and mobilisation	119
Transparency and fairness with suppliers	119
Value chain model	5
Value for money	7, 16
Vendor rating	68, 110
Web-based solutions	144
Weighted average	59
Work sampling	109
Zero defects	46, 86